Unl⊙ck

READING & WRITING SKILLS 5

Wendy Asplin and Carolyn Westbrook

CAMBRIDGE
UNIVERSITY PRESS

University Printing House, Cambridge CB2 8BS, United Kingdom

One Liberty Plaza, 20th Floor, New York, NY 10006, USA

477 Williamstown Road, Port Melbourne, VIC 3207, Australia

4843/24, 2nd Floor, Ansari Road, Daryaganj, Delhi – 110002, India

79 Anson Road, #06–04/06, Singapore 079906

Cambridge University Press is part of the University of Cambridge.

It furthers the University's mission by disseminating knowledge in the pursuit of education, learning and research at the highest international levels of excellence.

www.cambridge.org
Information on this title: www.cambridge.org/9781316647714

© Cambridge University Press 2017

This publication is in copyright. Subject to statutory exception and to the provisions of relevant collective licensing agreements, no reproduction of any part may take place without the written permission of Cambridge University Press.

First published 2017

20 19 18 17 16 15 14 13 12 11 10 9 8 7 6 5 4 3 2 1

Printed in China by CNPIEC Beijing Congreat Printing Co., Ltd.

A catalogue record for this publication is available from the British Library

ISBN 978-1-316-64771-4 Combined Skills 5 Workbook
ISBN 978-1-316-64770-7 Combined Skills 5 Student's Book

Additional resources for this publication at www.cambridge.org/unlock

Cambridge University Press has no responsibility for the persistence or accuracy of URLs for external or third-party internet websites referred to in this publication, and does not guarantee that any content on such websites is, or will remain, accurate or appropriate. Information regarding prices, travel timetables, and other factual information given in this work is correct at the time of first printing but Cambridge University Press does not guarantee the accuracy of such information thereafter.

CONTENTS

UNIT 1	Conservation	4
UNIT 2	Design	12
UNIT 3	Privacy	20
UNIT 4	Business	28
UNIT 5	Psychology	36
UNIT 6	Careers	46
UNIT 7	Health sciences	56
UNIT 8	Collaboration	66
UNIT 9	Technology	76
UNIT 10	Language	86
Acknowledgements		96

UNIT 1 CONSERVATION

READING

IDENTIFYING AN ARGUMENT

1 Read the essay and circle the sentence (a–e) that best describes the author's central claim.

   a Demolition of the empty buildings of Detroit is efficient and economical.
   b Preservation is good for the environment and economy of Detroit.
   c Developers are the key to revitalizing Detroit.
   d The revitalization of Detroit has been accomplished through preservation rather than demolition.
   e Detroit was a great city and has a rich history.

IDENTIFYING SUPPORTING DETAILS

2 Read the essay again. Tick ✔ the correct phrase (a–c) to complete each sentence (1–5). For some sentences, more than one answer is possible.

   1 Deconstruction is better than tearing down buildings because …
      a ☐ it is faster.
      b ✔ less material is thrown away.
      c ✔ it trains workers.

   2 The organization that does deconstruction of homes in Detroit …
      a ☐ sells the materials that are recovered.
      b ☐ rebuilds the homes.
      c ☐ uses the material to make new things.

   3 Many of the items recovered from a deconstructed home are …
      a ☐ historic.
      b ☐ unsafe.
      c ☐ vulnerable.

   4 Deconstructed home projects provide …
      a ☐ a new community.
      b ☐ jobs in the community.
      c ☐ opportunities to learn new job skills.

   5 Preservation of old buildings is important because …
      a ☐ they have historic and cultural value.
      b ☐ they draw visitors to the city.
      c ☐ it is not possible to create buildings like this again.

Detroit: Back from the ashes

Imagine a city with 78,000 vacant buildings: homes, office buildings, shops, hotels. This is what the city of Detroit, Michigan, recently faced. Once the fourth largest city in the United States, with a population of 2,000,000 people, Detroit was the car manufacturing capital of the world. Ford, General Motors and Chrysler all had headquarters there. After destructive riots in 1967, followed by competition from foreign car-makers in the 1970s, factories started to close, businesses folded and people moved away. In 2013, the population was just over 700,000, and empty buildings were everywhere.

Having so many abandoned buildings posed a huge problem for Detroit that had to be addressed. The buildings were unsafe, dirty and created a health hazard for communities. But not everyone agreed on how to deal with this problem. Developers believed that the most economical and efficient solution was to demolish the structures and rebuild with new buildings. Preservationists, on the other hand, saw opportunities to help the economy and the environment by working with communities to save entire or parts of valuable structures.

Thus far, approximately 7,000 buildings have been demolished. Most of that material has ended up in a dump, but starting in 2010, a non-profit group called Reclaim Detroit had a better idea. Their mission is deconstruction of buildings, not destruction. What does that mean? Instead of destruction, where buildings are quickly and completely torn down, the group employs people to deconstruct a building, slowly taking it apart and recovering materials that can be reused in new development. Each month, 10–20 abandoned homes are carefully deconstructed. They remove antique doors, windows, lighting fixtures, marble counters, bricks, nails and even wood flooring made from old-growth trees. From this recovered lumber, crews create new items like wooden cutting boards. Reclaim Detroit sells these items as well as many types of 'architectural salvage' on their website.

Deconstruction is good for the environment because less material goes to landfill, or dumps. It supports the community in providing jobs as well as job training for careers in construction. It also preserves historic architectural items.

Preservation of historic buildings is good for the city. Many of downtown Detroit's oldest and most beautiful buildings sat empty for decades. One of the city's oldest hotels, the Fort Shelby Hotel, closed in 1973 due to a lack of business. The Book-Cadillac, once a grand hotel serving presidents, film stars and sports heroes, closed its doors in 1984. These beautiful structures were then vulnerable to weather and vandalism. Rather than see them demolished, groups like Curbed Detroit and Preservation Detroit believed these and other grand buildings could be restored. In 2008, the Westin Book-Cadillac Detroit re-opened, and the Fort Shelby Hotel opened a few months later. Both of these historic buildings have been brought back to life.

The result has been good for tourism, as these classic hotels have attracted visitors to the city. Many tourists, as well as locals, enjoy historic tours of the city. These lovely restorations in the downtown core have also had a positive effect in encouraging other development. Most importantly, some of the history and culture of the city has been preserved. As Detroit preservationist Francis Grunow puts it, 'these buildings are works of art'. They cannot be recreated; they must be preserved.

The motto of the city expresses hope that Detroit will come back and prosper: *Speramus meliora; resurget cineribus.* 'We hope for better things; it will arise from the ashes.' Preservation plays an important part in that revitalization. It has an economic, environmental and cultural role in rebuilding this once great city.

MAKING INFERENCES FROM THE TEXT

3 Read the essay on page 5 again. Tick ✔ the correct box for each statement.

	true	false	does not say
1 Deconstruction takes more time than demolition.	✔		
2 Developers are not interested in the environmental issues in Detroit.			
3 Materials from deconstructed buildings can be used again.			
4 Developers prefer to tear down old buildings and build new ones because it is less costly.			
5 The historic hotels in Detroit were closed due to damage from weather and vandalism.			
6 Preservation of hotels has had positive economic effects in Detroit.			
7 Everyone who works with Reclaim Detroit is already highly trained in construction practices.			
8 Preservationists are business owners in the city.			

LANGUAGE DEVELOPMENT

UNIT VOCABULARY

4 Complete the sentences using words from the box. You do not need to use all the words.

> deliberate   maintained   prospered   prompted
> ~~vulnerable~~   emerged   recovered   deteriorated   vacant

1 Historic papers need to be preserved in low light because they are ___vulnerable___ to sunlight.
2 After a natural disaster, many historic items are lost forever and cannot be _____ .
3 Buildings that are _____ often attract criminal activity.
4 Reclaim Detroit made a _____ decision to save and reuse materials from old houses.
5 Preservationists have always _____ that saving historic buildings is a good idea economically.
6 When buildings have _____ too far, it may be impossible to restore them.
7 What _____ you to write to a newspaper about the demolition of old buildings in your town?

CONSERVATION — UNIT 1

5 Match the sentence halves.

___d___ 1 Because small towns don't have a lot of money,
_____ 2 Though it is valuable because it reminds us of our past,
_____ 3 Unlike preservationists,
_____ 4 As a very small company,
_____ 5 We were able to recover a lot of building material,
_____ 6 In order to be usable as a modern hospital again,
_____ 7 Though not usually done in the past,

a we don't have the capacity to take on more projects.
b a lot of memorabilia is not worth much money.
c the building needs to have a major renovation.
d big projects are often not affordable.
e developers like to bring change to a city.
f using old wooden floors in new buildings has become common practice.
g so we will need a huge storage facility.

TIME EXPRESSIONS

6 Find phrases in the box with the same meaning as the words in brackets. Complete the sentences using the phrases in the box.

> at one time   at the turn of the century
> for the time being   in the blink of an eye   it's about time
> over the past   ~~slowly but surely~~   up to date

1 ___Slowly but surely___ we accomplished our goal. (it took some time but)
2 We have continually made changes _____ year. (throughout the last)
3 It seems that, _____ , we can only sit and wait for the city council to make a decision. (for now)
4 _____ , international phone calls were very expensive, but not now. (in the past)
5 I didn't even see how the accident happened. Everything happened _____ . (really quickly)
6 You should rewrite your CV every year. It should always be _____ . (current)
7 _____ , people worried that all our computers would crash when we entered the year 2000. (in 1999)
8 After nearly five years under construction, _____ for the new bridge to open for public use. (now is finally the time)

COMPOUND ADJECTIVES

7 Circle the correct phrases to complete the sentences.

1 When artists restore old paintings, they use techniques that are (state of the art) / state-of-the-art.
2 Many works by *well known / well-known* artists like Michelangelo have been restored several times.
3 In Spain, a volunteer ruined a *centuries old / centuries-old* painting in a church when she tried to restore it.
4 While the *world famous / world-famous* Mona Lisa was being restored, a photographic copy replaced it in the Louvre.
5 At the Smithsonian, Xiangmei Gu restored Chinese paintings from the *twentieth century / twentieth-century* by first removing deteriorated paper.
6 At many museums, art conservation trainees study and work *part time / part-time*.

8 Complete the sentences using the compound adjectives in the box.

> low-income   well-known   ~~energy-efficient~~
> long-term   fast-growing

1 Developers are making use of new technologies as they design and build more ____energy-efficient____ homes.
2 There is a need for better public transportation systems in _____ cities.
3 As rents increase, big cities need to ensure that there are still good _____ housing options for their residents.
4 To solve big urban problems, cities need to think about the future and develop a good _____ plan.
5 Norman Foster is a _____ British architect whose work has won many prizes.

WRITING

FUTURE CONDITIONALS

9 Match the sentence halves.

__b__ 1 If the museum offers lectures about the history of the town's train station,
_____ 2 If we were to create shops and restaurants on the ground floor of the train station,
_____ 3 If we charge for tours of the building,
_____ 4 If the newspaper wrote a travel article about the station,
_____ 5 If we removed the antique ceiling,
_____ 6 If we use the upper levels for a luxury hotel,

a we would lose some of the historic feeling of the place.
b it will create public interest in restoring it.
c then we should employ professional guides.
d a lot of people will stay overnight.
e it would attract tourists from surrounding towns.
f this place could be as popular as the shopping centre!

10 Look at the pairs of sentences (1–5) and tick ✔ the sentence (a–b) in each pair that describes a more likely (less hypothetical) situation.

1 a ☐ If developers were to work with preservationists, both sides would be happier.
   b ✔ If developers work with preservationists, the resulting space is much more charming and beautiful.

2 a ☐ If the city bought the abandoned hotel, they would need to borrow money to renovate it.
   b ☐ If the city buys the hotel, they will partner with someone to restore it.

3 a ☐ If the citizens support the idea, it will be easy to convince the mayor.
   b ☐ If citizens supported the idea, the mayor would support it too.

4 a ☐ If a building is on the National Register of Historic Places, the city will not tear it down.
   b ☐ If this building were on the National Register of Historic Places, the city would never tear it down.

5 a ☐ If the university were to get involved, any decision we make would need approval by their board of governors.
   b ☐ If the university wants to get involved, they will have to help with the costs of construction.

IMPERSONAL STATEMENTS

11 Look at the pairs of sentences (1–7) and tick ✔ the sentence (a–b) in each pair that would be more appropriate for an academic paper.

1. a ☐ From my point of view, preserving antique cars is important from both a historic and a design perspective.
   b ✔ Because they are both historic and show design trends, it is important to preserve antique cars.

2. a ☐ With more interactive exhibits and less memorabilia, younger viewers would be more likely to visit museums.
   b ☐ It seems to me that museums would attract younger visitors if they had more interactive exhibits and less memorabilia.

3. a ☐ Cinemas like the old Globe Picture House should be preserved.
   b ☐ As far as I'm concerned, there is no reason to tear down the old Globe Picture House.

4. a ☐ The historic district is the most interesting part of a city.
   b ☐ In my opinion, historic districts are the most interesting areas in any city.

5. a ☐ I think old football stadiums should not be torn down, even when the city builds a new one.
   b ☐ When new stadiums are built, the older stadiums that they replace should not automatically be torn down.

6. a ☐ As I see it, the government should work with local businesses to save old structures.
   b ☐ Saving old structures requires that governments and local businesses work together.

7. a ☐ Only those buildings that are special in some way should be renovated.
   b ☐ We should only renovate the buildings that are special in some way.

PARAGRAPH STRUCTURE AND UNITY

12 Underline the topic sentence in each paragraph and cross out the sentences that do not belong in a unified paragraph.

> **Paragraph 1**
> In many cities, graffiti and painting on walls are considered vandalism and they are often painted over so that they are concealed. <u>On the tiny island of Malta, however, this kind of street art is actively encouraged.</u> ~~Malta was once a British colony but is now part of the European Union.~~ Surprisingly, there is a government agency on Malta that exists to support street art. The agency identifies public walls where such painting is allowed. These murals, or wall paintings, often reflect political and social issues on the island.

> **Paragraph 2**
> <u>Many argue that street art should be preserved, but even among the artists themselves there is no agreement on that issue.</u> On one side, people argue that street art is not meant to last. The art belongs to the street, and being painted over or destroyed is part of that street's lifecycle. ~~Of course, some art is more admired than other pieces and not everyone appreciates street art.~~ Others believe that works by famous artists, like Banksy or le Rat, should not be disturbed. They maintain that these images become an important part of a neighbourhood and should be preserved.

WRITING TASK

13 Imagine that your city government wants to spend taxpayer money to restore a historic train station in the city centre. Write a letter to the city council or a newspaper and make an argument for what you think should be done.

UNIT 2 DESIGN

READING

USING YOUR KNOWLEDGE

1 Read only the first and last paragraphs of the magazine article. Circle the most suitable title for the article.

   a The psychology of fonts
   b Designing fonts
   c Images and fonts in advertising

READING FOR DETAIL

2 Read the whole article and circle the correct words to complete the sentences.

   1 A designer working with a serious text would choose a *serif font / sans serif font / script font*.
   2 An ad for perfume might use a script font because it is *bold / trendy / feminine*.
   3 The participants in Errol Morris's study were people who *are interested in asteroids / read 'The New York Times' online / are interested in different fonts*.
   4 Morris's study showed that *people like the Baskerville font most / fonts affect believability / fonts can increase participation in surveys*.
   5 In Sarah Hyndman's study, participants were asked to *compare the flavour of two different jelly beans / rate the flavour of two identical jelly beans / indicate their preference for sweet or sour jelly beans*.
   6 Participants thought a jelly bean tasted more sour when *they were looking at a warm font / they were feeling angry / they were looking at a jagged font*.

A It's not hard to imagine having an emotional response to an ad with an image of a cute puppy or a stylish watch. It's also easy to recognize that certain colours in ads evoke certain emotions. Blue is calm and comforting, while red is exciting and bold. But most of us are not aware that we also react to the typeface – or font – that is used in an ad, a company logo, or even a newspaper story.

B Graphic designers know that fonts have personalities and gender. They have an emotional impact and can influence the reader. They are more than just letters on the page or screen, so designers choose carefully from thousands of fonts to send the right message. A serif font, like **Times New Roman**, with its small, extra lines that decorate each letter, is associated with respectability and tradition. It is serious and reliable and inspires confidence. By contrast, sans serif fonts lack these small, added lines, so they feel clean, modern and direct. These fonts also seem friendlier. The most recognizable is **Helvetica**, one of the most popular fonts in the world. Script fonts, like *Vivaldi*, resemble handwritten text and often feel feminine and personal, like an invitation. While a script font would not be appropriate for a bank contract, a serif font would probably not be a good choice to advertise perfume.

C How these fonts affect us may seem fairly obvious when they are pointed out. But what about our subconscious reactions to different fonts? Do we have responses that we are not even aware of? Several studies show that we do.

D In 2013, Errol Morris, a well-known documentary filmmaker and writer, learned that the believability of an article is related to the font that is used. He did an experiment through a newspaper, *The New York Times*, in which he asked online readers to read a passage about the unlikely possibility of Earth being destroyed by an asteroid. Readers were then asked to complete a survey. Nearly 45,000 people responded. Each participant read the passage in one of six different fonts: **Baskerville**, Computer Modern, **Georgia**, **Helvetica**, **Trebuchet**, or **Comic Sans**. Participants were then asked whether they thought the information in the article was true. It turned out that the article was most believable to those who had read it in the Baskerville font.

E Could fonts also affect how things taste to us? Sarah Hyndman, a graphic designer, worked with researchers from Oxford University to find out. She wanted to show how fonts affect consumer behaviour. In her study, she gave each participant two jelly beans that were the same flavour. As they ate the first jelly bean, they looked at the words 'eat me' written in a soft, rounded font, one that was very friendly and warm. Then they rated the taste of the jelly bean: sweet, sour, or bitter. Next, they ate and rated the second jelly bean while they looked at the same words in a jagged, sharp, angular font, which Hyndman describes as 'angry'. When participants were looking at the soft, rounded font, they rated the jelly bean 17% sweeter. The same jelly bean was rated 11% more sour when they were looking at the jagged font. Hyndman believes that the font used on packaging may affect the perceived sweetness or saltiness of the food consumers enjoy.

F Fonts are everywhere in our world. We see them on buses, magazine covers and food packaging. Those fonts have a personality and a message, and we have a reaction to them, both consciously and subconsciously. The next time you are walking down a street, notice the fonts around you. Think about how you feel or what the designer might have intended. Who knows – maybe your lunch will taste better!

MAKING INFERENCES

3 Read the statements (1–6) and decide whether you can infer them from the magazine article on page 13. Tick ✔ the correct box for each statement.

	yes	no
1 Many people do not notice the design of written words.	✔	
2 A sans serif font would appeal to people who enjoy things that are new or trendy.		
3 Designers spend a lot of time creating new fonts.		
4 Most newspapers are written in Baskerville font.		
5 Readers would be less likely to trust an article written in Comic Sans.		
6 Fonts could help guide people toward healthier food choices.		

LANGUAGE DEVELOPMENT

UNIT VOCABULARY

4 Circle the correct words to complete the paragraph.

Many common products may not be ⁽¹⁾*devoted to / appropriate for* some elderly people. Something as simple as buttoning a shirt can be difficult for them. To address this problem, one designer ⁽²⁾*modified / evolved* buttons by adding a narrow piece that slips easily into the buttonhole. Designers also made changes to phones by adding bright colours and large numbers on the keypad, which ⁽³⁾*appeal to / resemble* people who can't see well. Many older people ⁽⁴⁾*resist / opt for* buying certain products for the elderly because they're not attractive. As a result, designers have begun to create stylish and ⁽⁵⁾*contemporary / subsequent* designs for products aimed at older people. These fashionable products no longer need to be ⁽⁶⁾*retained / associated* with being old.

5 Complete the text using the words in the box.

> criteria   resemble   devoted   donations
> human rights   subsequent   evolved

The Bill & Melinda Gates Foundation is (1)_____ to finding solutions to big, global problems. They give money to many organizations, including many that fight for education, healthcare and other (2)_____ for the poor. The money comes only from the Gates family – they do not take (3)_____ from the public.

In 2011, the Foundation held a competition for a new toilet design for developing countries. There were several (4)_____ for the new design, such as no connection to water or electricity, and the need to produce useful resources from the waste. There were 29 designs submitted, and the Foundation held a design fair in Seattle in 2012 to show them to the world.

In (5)_____ years, there were more competitions with fairs held in other countries. As for the toilets, the original designs have (6)_____ over the years as more designers have got involved. Sometimes they (7)_____ little factories or machines.

COLLOCATIONS TO DESCRIBE EMOTIONAL RESPONSES

6 Complete the sentences using the verbs in the box.

> stir up   inspire   provoke   arouse   evoke   generate

1 Certain smells, like holiday foods, can _____ memories from childhood.
2 Good online reviews will usually _____ confidence in a new product.
3 Marketing teams often start a new project with a brainstorming session, hoping that this will _____ ideas that they can develop into full campaigns.
4 Some professors like to make statements that _____ controversy so students will react and respond.
5 A bag left at an airport terminal will probably _____ suspicion.
6 A rude comment on social media can _____ trouble.

PARAPHRASING

7 Match the sentences (1–4) with their paraphrases (a–d).

1 Students in graphic design programmes often create their own fonts.
2 New font designs are constantly being created.
3 These days it is very easy for anyone with a computer to create their own original font.
4 Many of the fonts that come already installed on computers are the most widely used now.

a Artists regularly create new fonts.
b Designing new fonts is common in graphic arts classes.
c The most popular fonts are the ones that are part of a computer's regular font menu.
d New fonts can be easily created nowadays with the aid of technology.

8 Read the sentences (1–3) and tick ✔ the better paraphrase (a–b) for each sentence.

1 Steve Jobs's interest in design was inspired by the simple modern design of the homes in the neighbourhood he grew up in.
   a ☐ The style of the houses in Steve Jobs's childhood community influenced his love of design.
   b ☐ Steve Jobs's design interest was motivated by the houses in the neighbourhood where he grew up.

2 He loved simplicity in design and he wanted a clean look for his product, so he chose white for the iPhone.
   a ☐ He selected white for the iPhone because he liked simplicity of design and he liked a clean look.
   b ☐ He wanted the iPhone to be streamlined and white because he valued designs that were simple and looked clean.

3 'The main thing in our design is that we have to make things intuitively obvious,' Jobs said.
   a ☐ Jobs said that the most important thing about the design is that it had to be 'intuitively obvious'.
   b ☐ Jobs said that the design is the main thing because it's obvious.

WRITING

NON-DEFINING RELATIVE CLAUSES

9 Rewrite the sentences to include the additional information as a non-defining relative clause. Be sure to punctuate your sentences correctly.

1 Fonts have become widely used in home publishing.
   Additional information: Fonts are now free on computers.
   Fonts, which are now free on computers, have become widely used in home publishing.

2 National highway signs must be easy to read.
   Additional information: These signs are in Highway Gothic font.

3 Trendy fonts appeal to younger readers.
   Additional information: Trendy fonts are simple and clean.

4 Market research shows that a very small font can influence people to buy a product.
   Additional information: A very small font is hard to read.

5 Fun fonts can evoke feelings of joy and happiness.
   Additional information: Fun fonts are often silly and colourful.

APPOSITIVES

10 Rewrite each pair of sentences (1–4) as one sentence, using an appositive.

1 Kevin Larson is a researcher at Microsoft. He works to improve the quality of on-screen text.
Kevin Larson, _____a researcher at Microsoft_____ , works to improve the quality of on-screen text.

2 Comic Sans was designed for children, but it is popular with adults as well. Comic Sans is a sans serif script font.
The _____ was designed for children, but it is popular with adults as well.

3 In 2015, *The New York Times* changed its font to Georgia because it is easier to read. *The New York Times* is a highly respected newspaper.
In 2015, *The New York Times*, _____ , changed its font to Georgia because it is easier to read.

4 Reading speed and comprehension are improved when computers use Clear Type. Clear Type is a font improvement technology.
Reading speed and comprehension are improved when computers use Clear Type, _____ .

CONCLUSIONS

11 Read the paragraph below, which is the conclusion of the article on page 13. Underline the phrase that expresses the main idea of the article. Underline the sentence(s) that give the reader something new to think about.

> Fonts are everywhere in our world. We see them on buses, magazine covers and food packaging. Those fonts have a personality and a message, and we have a reaction to them, both consciously and subconsciously. The next time you are walking down a street, notice the fonts around you. Think about how you feel or what the designer might have intended. Who knows – maybe your lunch will taste better!

WRITING A SUMMARY–RESPONSE ESSAY

12 Read paragraphs B and D on page 13 again, and look at 1–4 below. For each paragraph, write *S* for the best summary and *R* for the best response.

Paragraph B

1 Fonts affect readers and the fonts that designers choose can influence how readers feel and react. Serif, sans serif and script fonts all have a different impact. _____

2 There are many different kinds of fonts and the most respected one is Times New Roman. Helvetica is the most popular. All of them influence us in a different way. _____

3 People in marketing always try to take advantage of consumers and this is another example of that. People are being influenced by fonts but they don't even realize it. _____

4 This indicates that fonts have more power than people realize. Studies show that handwritten fonts on junk mail fool people into opening those letters because they look personal. _____

Paragraph D

1 If I owned a newspaper, I would use Baskerville font for the news. People want to trust their news and that would build trust in the newspaper. _____

2 The results are very interesting, but they may be unreliable. Another study with a larger number of fonts could confirm these results. _____

3 Baskerville font is the most believable font, based on a study by *The New York Times*. People didn't really trust Computer Modern, Georgia, Helvetica, Trebuchet or Comic Sans fonts. _____

4 An online experiment showed that a font can affect the believability of a newspaper article. Those who read the article written in Baskerville font were more likely to believe the information than those who read it in the other five fonts used in the experiment. _____

WRITING TASK

13 Write a summary–response essay for the magazine article on page 13.

UNIT 3   PRIVACY

READING

IDENTIFYING MAIN IDEAS

1 Read the article. Match the main ideas (1–6) with paragraphs of the article (A–F).

___C___ 1 Many internet users do not take responsibility for protecting their data.

_____ 2 The education of children should include classes about online privacy.

_____ 3 The concept of privacy has changed in recent years.

_____ 4 The government has a responsibility to help protect personal data.

_____ 5 Personal information about people is regularly being collected and sold.

_____ 6 Workshops in community centres can help people learn how to protect their privacy better.

IDENTIFYING SUPPORTING DETAILS

2 Read the article again. Tick ✔ the correct box for each statement.

	true	false
1 Internet users are told when their personal data is sold to an advertiser.		
2 Most secondary school students are aware of how to handle their online privacy.		
3 According to the author, online safety should begin in secondary school.		
4 The US has very few laws relating to data protection.		
5 In the UK, companies are punished if they do not tell customers quickly that their data was stolen.		
6 The US is working very quickly to introduce laws like those in the UK.		

Protecting your privacy: Whose job is it?

A Most people who grew up in the 20th century expected privacy. They could be reasonably sure that when they left their homes, no one was tracking them. Generally, what they bought and where they went and whom they associated with were not known outside of their families, friends and maybe business associates. But all of that changed in the century that followed. With the internet came a new definition of privacy and, along with it, a number of disturbing problems.

B Today, there is no guarantee of privacy when a person visits a website or uses an app. Personal habits and interests are all tracked each time a person goes online or swipes a credit card. It's as if a person leaves a sticky note everywhere they go, and a data analyst walks behind them gathering these bits of information to create a profile about that person. That profile is then sold to anyone who wants it. Information like this is valuable to advertisers because they can direct specific ads to someone based on personal information. Most people are unaware of what others know about them.

C Part of the problem lies with us. Beginning in the early 2000s, with the popularity of social media, users shared all kinds of personal information, often without any privacy settings. Even today, though people take care to lock their cars and houses, many take no steps at all to protect their privacy online. Identity theft is one of the fastest-growing crimes across the world, affecting millions of people every year.

D To address this growing problem, schools need to include online safety as part of the curriculum. This training should begin at a very young age, when students are learning what personal information actually is. Older students should be taught why protecting their data is important, as well as how to control at least some of their personal information. These days, it is assumed that millennials know how to control privacy settings, but recent studies have shown that many do not.

E Internet users who are not tech-savvy may not know where to start to protect their data. Libraries and community centres often offer workshops. Personal cyber-security can start with something as basic as making sure to block access to electronic devices with a screen lock. Julia Angwin, an award-winning reporter at ProPublica, says that there are plenty of simple, cheap and effective steps that can be taken to protect privacy online, such as updating software regularly and putting tape over a laptop camera – something that even Mark Zuckerberg of Facebook does. While these steps will not completely eliminate the problem, teaching users these simple tools gives them some control over their privacy.

F While users can and should take some responsibility for protecting their privacy, a large part of the solution must come from governments. The United States, for example, has been very slow to adopt data protection laws, and those that exist today are extremely limited. To really confront this threat, existing laws in the US need to be expanded, giving people the right to control their own data. In Europe and Canada there are laws that regulate how personal data can be used. Under a law in the European Union called 'the right to be forgotten', individuals can request that search engines like Google remove links to news articles in the British press. Laws also require that customers be notified within three days when personal data is stolen, with a penalty for companies that don't comply. Furthermore, a company must supply the details of any personal data they hold upon that person's request. These and similar laws need to be enacted in many more countries before cyber-security problems get any worse.

G Privacy and security online will remain issues for some time, but for now, it takes the concerted effort of users, teachers, community groups and governments to find workable solutions.

PURPOSE AND TONE

3 Read the article on page 21 again. Tick ✔ the correct answer (a–d) to each question.

1 Which idea best describes the author's main purpose for writing this article?
   a ☐ to teach people how to protect their privacy online
   b ☐ to suggest ideas that address the problem of protecting personal data
   c ☐ to encourage governments to pass more laws related to protecting personal data
   d ☐ to explain why protecting personal information is important

2 Which phrase best describes the author's tone?
   a ☐ informative and concerned
   b ☐ neutral and objective
   c ☐ humorous and entertaining
   d ☐ casual and light-hearted

LANGUAGE DEVELOPMENT

UNIT VOCABULARY

4 Complete the paragraphs using the words in the box.

> humiliation   guarantee   regulate   penalty
> prosecute   disturbing   eliminate   malicious

The use of personal drones has become an issue of privacy. For many people, the idea of a tiny camera taking pictures of them in their backyard or garden is (1)_____ . Embarrassing photos can be shared online, which could result in (2)_____ for an innocent person.

Several places (3)_____ personal drones by limiting them to airspace over 500 feet. This does not (4)_____ the problem, however, because the cameras are still able to take photos so the ruling does not (5)_____ personal privacy. Recently, a homeowner felt that a drone had violated the privacy of his teenage daughter who was sunbathing in the garden, so he shot the aircraft down. Many others have done the same when they felt drones were spying on them. But using a gun in this way is a crime in most places, and the (6)_____ can include a large fine or even a prison sentence.

Most drone operators just enjoy taking photos from the air and are not (7)_____ , but some are careless and dangerous. When a drone pilot intentionally causes harm to others, law enforcement can take steps to (8)_____ them for their actions.

5 Circle the correct words to complete the sentences.

1 Some medical researchers worry that privacy laws about health data are a *barrier / guarantee* to sharing information with other scientists.
2 These scientists insist that the data that they share is *abusive / anonymous* and is not associated with the names of any patients.
3 Several employees at one big hospital were *prosecuted / eliminated* for secretly looking through the medical records of celebrities.
4 All of the employees who were involved were *suspended / assembled*.
5 In addition, the hospital had to pay a large *humiliation / penalty*.
6 In a separate case, a nurse went to prison after she posted *disturbing / abusive* photos on social media of elderly patients.

COLLOCATIONS OF BEHAVIOUR

6 Complete the sentences using the words in the box.

> abuse   confidence   behaviour   responsibility   pain   a reputation

1 Many people believe that they must take _____ for protecting their own personal data.
2 This is partly because they have lost _____ in companies to keep their data private.
3 Germany has built _____ for having very strict privacy laws.
4 For a short time, South Korea tried to implement a 'real names policy' because they believed this would ensure more polite _____ online.
5 In all cultures, there are people who experience _____ online.
6 In general, people who are attacked online suffer a lot of _____ from this type of abuse.

COLLOCATIONS FOR STATING THE EXISTENCE OF PROBLEMS

7 Circle the correct words to complete the sentences.

1 The paparazzi – aggressive photographers and journalists who chase celebrities – can *face / present* problems for innocent bystanders on the street.
2 The paparazzi's careless behaviour has *run into / become* an issue because it has caused serious accidents.
3 They not only invade the privacy of a celebrity, they also *face / represent* a threat to public safety.
4 Their actions are legal as long as they stay in public areas, so they only *run into / present* trouble with the police when they damage property or hurt people.
5 Just going out for a walk *faces / presents* a challenge for many celebrities who have paparazzi waiting outside their homes all day and all night.
6 Some celebrities believe that drones *cause / pose* a risk to their families.

COLLOCATIONS FOR DESCRIBING SOLUTIONS

8 Match the sentence halves.

_____ 1 Laws that make it illegal to photograph the children of famous people
_____ 2 Michael Jackson addressed the threat to his children's privacy
_____ 3 After many car accidents, some governments are confronting the problem
_____ 4 Unfortunately, most of these laws do not really resolve the issue,

a by prosecuting paparazzi who cause crashes.
b because the paparazzi are still causing accidents.
c try to protect the privacy of innocent family members.
d by covering their faces when they went out.

WRITING

IMPERSONAL PASSIVES

9 Rewrite the sentences (1–5) in two ways, using the impersonal passive.

1 Everyone believes that the stealing of personal data is a serious problem.
   The stealing of personal data is believed to be a serious problem. / It is believed that the stealing of personal data is a serious problem.

2 People expect that privacy laws protect internet users.

3 People believe that governments are too slow to act on this problem.

4 People say that companies collect too much personal data.

5 People think that the elderly are even more vulnerable than children on the internet.

PASSIVES FOR CONTINUITY

10 Rewrite the sentences (1–5) so that the second clause uses the passive. Omit the *by* phrase if it is not necessary.

1 When large amounts of data are analyzed, analysts can use them to predict buying behaviour. When large amounts of data are analyzed, _they can be used to predict buying behaviour_.

2 Although drones may be useful, people view them as dangerous toys. Although drones may be useful, _____.

3 If a company in the EU violates privacy laws, regulators can issue penalties that amount to as much as 250,000 euros. If a company in the EU violates privacy laws, _____.

4 Though companies can monitor employees, the law requires companies to inform employees in advance. Though companies can monitor employees, _____.

5 Because a National Insurance number is very useful to criminals, people in the UK consider it very sensitive data. Because a National Insurance number is very useful to criminals, _____.

WRITING ABOUT PROBLEMS

11 Read the description of a problem. Tick ✔ the correct box for each sentence in the table below.

(a)Privacy in the workplace has become an issue in recent years. (b)More and more large companies are spying on their employees. (c)A recent study revealed that as many as 60% of companies in the UK monitor their employees' internet use, emails, or phone calls. (d)In one case, an employee removed a tracking app from her work phone because she did not want to be tracked outside of work and was fired the following week. (e)Is this kind of spying even necessary? (f)At the very least, workers should not be monitored or tracked in their free time. (g)This problem will probably continue to grow as more tools become available to spy on employees.

		fact	example	statistic	opinion
1	sentence b	✔			
2	sentence c				
3	sentence d				
4	sentence f				

WRITING ABOUT SOLUTIONS

12 Read the description of a solution. Tick ✔ the correct box for each sentence in the table below.

> (a)Surveys show that most employees do not believe they are being spied on, or that their company has a right to spy on them. (b)It's clear that companies should tell employees that they are being tracked and ask them to agree to that. (c)It is also generally assumed that a company has no right to keep track of an employee when they are not at work. (d)However, many do. (e)While it's not true everywhere, several countries have laws that do not allow employers to track employees in non-working hours. (f)Employees need to learn what their rights are and be sure their employers respect their right to privacy.

		research cited by author	generally held view	direct suggestion
1	sentence a			
2	sentence b			
3	sentence c			
4	sentence f			

WRITING TASK

13 Write a problem–solution essay about a privacy issue in your school, neighbourhood or workplace.

UNIT 4 BUSINESS

READING

SCANNING

1 Scan the article and match each item of information (1–7) with the paragraph (A–G) in which it can be found. You will find that one paragraph can match with two items.

_____ 1 A description of utilitarian marketing
_____ 2 Suggestions for ways that marketing teams can change from traditional to utilitarian marketing
_____ 3 Examples of people sharing their own ideas about something
_____ 4 An explanation of different ways to use content
_____ 5 Ways that billboards are designed to be a utility
_____ 6 Information to show why direct marketing doesn't work
_____ 7 Different ways that companies have created apps to be utilities

READING FOR MAIN IDEAS

2 Read the article again. Tick ✔ the statements that support the main ideas.

a ☐ Advertising is not effective.
b ☐ Utilitarian marketing is about providing something useful that people need.
c ☐ Traditional marketing does not have a future.
d ☐ Selling to people is not part of utilitarian marketing.
e ☐ Utilitarian marketing builds long-term brand loyalty.
f ☐ People are always willing to share their ideas about products.

SELL MORE BY SELLING LESS

A   Consider this statistic: in any given day, the average person may be exposed to as many as 5,000 marketing messages. With so much direct advertising and brand reminders, from TV to email sales pitches to targeted online ads, how much attention do people really pay to these messages? Apparently, not much. One study indicates that only 12 messages actually reach us. And what is the result? A public who is tired of ads and even more tired of constantly being sold to. Yet marketers continue to fill the public's focus with ads. Isn't there a better way?

B   Mitch Joel thinks so. As president of a digital marketing agency, he has moved towards a different way to connect to customers: utilitarian marketing. Rather than advertising – which focuses on how great a product is – utilitarian marketing focuses on understanding what the customer needs and then providing something of true value; something that solves a problem, something that makes their lives easier. In other words, a utility, something a customer can use. This, he says, leads to brand loyalty.

C   Jay Baer, a marketing consultant, agrees, 'If you sell something, you make a customer today. If you help someone, you make a customer for life.' In his best-selling book, *Youtility*, Baer argues that – contrary to traditional marketing strategies – offering something that is both useful and free will build long-term trust with a customer. Long-term loyalty will outweigh short-term returns on investment. For some, utility is a powerful incentive to stay loyal to a brand.

D   Mobile apps are one way that companies can offer utility. SitOrSquat is an app that was created by the company that makes Charmin, a brand of very soft toilet paper. The app shows where a person can find clean public toilets. Users can add their own comments and even photos. There is no ad saying how soft the toilet paper is, just directions to the toilets of the users' choice. Similarly, the insurance company Nationwide has created an app that solves a very stressful problem: what to do after a car accident. The app tells users exactly what steps to take at the accident site, locates nearby towing services, and even includes a torch. Neither app tries to sell a product; they just offer something people could use.

E   Companies can also provide utility through content. Brian Sutter, a marketing specialist, encourages companies to teach rather than sell. He urges them to create content that is generous, honest and useful. Unlike an advertising campaign, Sutter says there should be no sales pitch of any kind. In fact, he suggests that a company does not even mention its products and services, or how to buy them, but just includes its logo. That means that a company doesn't shrewdly include its marketing message in its utility. The content can be as small as cooking demos and free recipe cards at supermarkets, to more elaborate how-to videos from hardware stores or educational webinars from textbook publishers. While customers may buy ingredients from the supermarket, supplies from the hardware store, or textbooks from the publisher, they are not actively being sold to.

F   Another way of adding value is through real-time social response, where the utility comes from the users. IBM did this with a clever ad campaign that encouraged participation in a worldwide dialogue for its 'People for Smarter Cities' initiative. The public was invited to contribute their ideas about how to make cities better. IBM got people's attention through simple billboards that were also designed to be something useful in the city: a bench, a rain shelter, or a ramp. The billboards themselves were utilities, as was the online discussion that resulted. In a very different campaign, instead of marketing its stain removal product in a traditional way, Vanish did something unusual. It invited people to share their own ideas about removing stains. This collection of people's own solutions became the basis of the Tip Exchange, an ongoing discussion forum on the company's website.

G   Utilitarian marketing works, but it requires a change of thinking for most marketing teams. To help make the transition, Ekaterina Walter, a marketing innovator and social media strategist for big companies, offers these tips:
- know what your customers need
- think about service before marketing
- make loyalty the goal instead of sales
- understand that your work is for the long term

Basically, companies need to give in order to get. As Walter says, utilitarian marketing is all about heart.

MAKING INFERENCES

3 Read the statements (1–7) and decide whether you can infer them from article on page 29. Tick ✔ the correct box for each statement.

	yes	no
1 Utilitarian marketing is expensive.		
2 It is not easy for traditional marketing teams to change the way they do marketing.		
3 Utilities should be available and free to everyone.		
4 People don't notice most of the advertising around them.		
5 Utilitarian marketing is more popular with young people.		
6 It takes more time to create a utilitarian marketing campaign.		
7 For traditional advertisers, sales are more important than long-term loyalty.		

LANGUAGE DEVELOPMENT

UNIT VOCABULARY

4 Complete the text using words from the box. You do not need to use all the words.

> ongoing   aspiring   fluctuates   retention   incentive
> proposition   outweighs   transition   pioneer   attainable

After watching her parents struggle with their small business for 30 years, Danae Ringelmann was inspired to create Indiegogo, a site that joins entrepreneurs to people with funds to invest. She became a (1)_____ in the online crowdfunding movement.

(2)_____ filmmakers and artists use crowdfunding sites like Indiegogo or GoFundMe to raise money for specific projects – finishing production on an independent film, or publishing a book of photography. Crowdfunding can also be used for (3)_____ projects, such as an annual arts festival that needs new funding each year. For those types of projects, the (4)_____ of donors from year to year is important.

These days, some start-ups generate interest in their ideas through online crowdfunding sites like Kickstarter, where supporters donate money in exchange for a small reward. Many start-ups feel that the attention their product gets on a crowdfunding site (5)_____ the risk of having their ideas stolen. To start a campaign, a team needs to decide on a financial target that is (6)_____ ; if they don't reach their target, they don't get any of the donations. They also need to choose a good (7)_____ to encourage people to donate money, such as discounts or a special backstage tour.

5 Circle the correct words and phrases to complete the sentences.

1 Because of high start-up costs, many businesses do not make a profit but they may *break even / fluctuate* in their first year.
2 There are many *transitions / components* to a business plan, including a plan for how to deliver a company's message.
3 *Revenue / Retention* from a crowdfunding campaign is helpful for new businesses that can't get traditional loans from banks.
4 Some companies *shrewdly / transitionally* place their products in films or TV programmes as a form of suggestive advertising. Few viewers even realize it.
5 To attract investors, a business owner needs to have a good business *pioneer / proposition* that includes a multi-year plan for the future of the company.
6 If a new business *outweighs / accumulates* too much debt, it may not be able to attract new investors easily.

EXPRESSING CONTRAST

6 Complete the paragraph using the words and phrases in the box.

> unlike   in contrast   rather   instead of   in spite of

Patagonia and North Face both sell top quality outdoor equipment. (1)_____ this basic similarity, their business models could not be more different. (2)_____ the typical growth model pursued by North Face, Patagonia actually wants to limit growth and make less money. In 2013, North Face earned £1.6 billion. (3)_____ , Patagonia only made £460 million. North Face wants to continue to expand its fashionable urban label, (4)_____ the founder of Patagonia, Yvon Chouinard, who wants to sell less. He believes that consumers should buy less for environmental reasons. His marketing campaign does not encourage customers to buy a new jacket just because it looks cool. (5)_____ , he hopes customers will buy a new jacket only because they need one.

7 Circle the correct words and phrases to complete the sentences.

1 *Instead of / In contrast / Unlike* traditional marketing, utilitarian marketing offers customers something they need.
2 *On the other hand / Rather than / In contrast* selling to customers, utilitarian marketing solves a problem for them.
3 *Rather than / Despite / In fact* the amount of advertising they see, only 1% of millennials – people born near the start of this century – say they are influenced by it.
4 Many believe that millennials are not loyal to brands; *instead of / in fact / in spite of*, they are the most brand-loyal generation ever.
5 Millennials can choose from a wide variety of products, *in contrast / however / yet* they stay loyal to brands that deliver quality experiences.
6 Millennials consider brand reputation when they try a new product; *however, / in contrast to / rather than* they are generally more influenced by the recommendation of a friend.

BUSINESS AND MARKETING VOCABULARY

8 Match the sentence halves.

_____ 1 Recently, home gardeners and bakers have started to sell at farmers' markets
_____ 2 For very low start-up costs of
_____ 3 Despite that, it takes time to know what will sell well,
_____ 4 A person selling homemade pies, for example, may not be able to produce enough to sell to a large supermarket chain,
_____ 5 Some established vendors use farmers' markets as a way to advertise their brand
_____ 6 These types of vendors usually sell sample products
_____ 7 At farmers' markets, vendors who sell inexpensive like pies and pizzas are usually very busy. Their costs are low,
_____ 8 The people who organize farmers' markets want successful vendors, large or small;

a that are regularly available in their nearby brick-and-mortar stores.
b as a result, they try to keep those who have a good track record.
c just a small rental fee and a business licence, a vendor can get started.
d but at a farmers' market they can run a business on a small scale.
e so they almost always make a profit.
f and consider farmers' markets to be a valuable marketing tool for them.
g so that they can generate a little extra revenue for themselves.
h so in the first few months, some people just break even at the market.

WRITING

REDUCING SUBORDINATE CLAUSES

9 Tick ✔ the sentences in which the subordinate clause could be reduced.

- a ☐ While they were trying to get a taxi in the snow in Paris in 2008, Travis Kalanick and Garrett Camp came up with the idea for Uber.
- b ☐ Once the app was launched in San Francisco, people quickly started to see the value of being able to request a car with a few taps on their smartphones.
- c ☐ Since he was encouraged by his early success, Kalanick started expanding into other cities.
- d ☐ Because drivers are allowed to choose when they work, they usually stick with the job.
- e ☐ While this sharing economy is allowing drivers to earn some extra income, some city officials worry about the lack of safety regulations for this industry.
- f ☐ If passengers are given a choice, they will usually choose the cheapest service.
- g ☐ As more and more users adopt on-demand services, developers are creating new online companies and services to satisfy them.

10 For each sentence, rewrite the subordinate clause in brackets as a reduced clause.

1 (Because they were unable to pay their rent in San Francisco in 2007), two flatmates decided to rent out space in their loft – that was the start of Airbnb.
   Unable to pay their rent in San Francisco in 2007, two flatmates decided to rent out space in their loft – that was the start of Airbnb.

2 _____
   (When they were initially rejected by investors), they decided to join another team who helped them redesign and perfect their product.

3 _____
   (Since they were aware that professional photographs attract more business), they employed photographers to take top quality photos of each place for the Airbnb website.

4 _____
   (If they are satisfied with their experience), many guests remain loyal Airbnb customers.

5 _____
   (As it is expanding into many different areas), the sharing economy is changing how people travel, drive, or even do household chores.

COMPARE AND CONTRAST ESSAY

11 Read the essays and circle the correct organizational pattern for each one.

1 *Point-by-point organization / Block organization*

> Today's millennials are comfortable buying everything online, from shoes to cars. They even like grocery shopping online, although many also like shopping at a brick-and-mortar supermarket. How do these experiences differ?
>
> There is no question that online grocery shopping is convenient. It saves a great deal of time, including driving to the supermarket and queuing during busy periods. It can also be a more affordable option, since prices are kept low and there are often online deals available, though one should be aware of delivery fees. While a shopper cannot choose the actual items purchased, businesses make every effort to send high-quality groceries.
>
> Shopping in a supermarket is a completely different experience. During very busy periods, especially at weekends, it can take a great deal of time just to go through the checkout. However, for shoppers who enjoy looking at new products or who like to walk down every aisle to get ideas, shopping at supermarkets is ideal. For cooks who are very picky about how ripe the avocado is or the freshness of the lettuce, the supermarket is the only option.

2 *Point-by-point organization / Block organization*

> Today's millennials are comfortable buying everything online, from shoes to cars. They even like grocery shopping online, although there is still a place for shopping at a brick-and-mortar supermarket. How do these experiences differ?
>
> Probably the biggest difference is the opportunity for a customer to touch, smell and see what they are buying. This is especially an issue with produce or items like fish or meat. Online, one must trust someone else to select those items.
>
> Another big difference is time. Just going to the supermarket takes time, even if it is close to home. In contrast, online shopping can be done whenever it is convenient – even in the middle of the night – and it only takes a few minutes.
>
> One other difference is impulse buying – decisions to buy something in the moment, something that catches the shopper's eye. Online shoppers are much less likely to be tempted to buy something usually found only at the checkout in a brick-and-mortar store, like chocolate bars and gossip magazines.

12 Complete the outline for each essay type using the phrases in the box.

> Limited direct sales at pop-up shop but good for exposure
> How employees are different between a pop-up shop and a traditional shop
> How costs of pop-up shops and traditional shops differ
> Costs of maintaining a traditional shop

Topic: Compare and contrast pop-up shops and traditional shops

Block organization
First paragraph: Cost of building and running a pop-up shop
                   (1)_____

Second paragraph: Temporary workers in pop-up shops
                   (2)_____
                   Ongoing sales with regular customers in traditional shop
                   Long-term staff in traditional shops

Point-by-point organization
First paragraph: (3)_____
Second paragraph: Differences in customer experiences in a pop-up shop and a traditional shop
Third paragraph: (4)_____

WRITING TASK

13 Write an essay that compares and contrasts the customer experience of shopping online with that of shopping in a brick-and-mortar store.
OR
Write an essay that compares and contrasts the customer experience in the sharing economy and the traditional service economy – for example, Uber vs. a licensed taxi, or Airbnb vs. a hotel.

UNIT 5 PSYCHOLOGY

READING

PREDICTING CONTENT

1 Read only the title and the first sentence from each paragraph in the article. Based on that information, circle the sentence (a–d) that best describes the main idea of the article.

   a Human brains may have undiscovered creative genius.
   b Creative geniuses are born, not made.
   c Acquired savants suffer when their genius is uncovered.
   d People who are geniuses have brain damage.

USING GRAPHIC ORGANIZERS

2 Read the article and tick ✔ the correct box for each theory (1–7).

	Treffert	Brogaard	Treffert and Brogaard
1 The healthy half of the brain will become more active to help the injured half.			
2 Magnetic stimulation to the brain can reveal artistic ability.			
3 We all have dormant creative potential.			
4 Non-invasive methods can help access creative genius.			
5 Chemicals that are released in an injury change the brain.			
6 Drugs and technology can help access creative genius.			
7 Technology may not be the best choice for accessing the brain.			

THE ACCIDENTAL GENIUS

Mozart was born a musical genius, composing music at the age of five. The genius of Galileo, who changed the way we think about our universe, was evident at a young age. Bobby Fischer, whom many consider the greatest chess player of all time, showed talent when he was very young. These and many like them were born with a rare talent. But not all geniuses have these skills from birth. In fact, some become geniuses quite literally by accident!

In 2002, Jason Padgett was an average 31-year-old who had dropped out of university and had never studied any maths at a higher level than basic algebra. One night, as he left a bar, he was attacked and severely beaten, which resulted in a serious brain injury. What happened next was intriguing. He became obsessed with numbers, geometry and formulas. In fact, he became a mathematical genius. He began drawing beautiful, intricate geometric shapes that are visual representations of mathematical structures, which is how he now sees the world. In 2016, Padgett explained, 'For me, pi was a shape that you could represent with a number, but I didn't know how to calculate it … All I knew was how to draw it. We're not wired to see things as digits or as numbers. We're wired to see things as shapes.'

Padgett is an acquired savant – a person who becomes a genius in one particular area after a severe brain trauma. This condition is rare, with only about 50 confirmed cases. What is common to all of them is that they are suddenly able to do something exceptionally well after a serious injury or illness. Their genius is often artistic, musical, mathematical, or related to memory. After Derek Amato smashed his head against the concrete floor of a swimming pool, he developed a phenomenal talent for playing complex piano pieces. After a series of severe epileptic seizures, Daniel Tammet's memory became extraordinary. He was able to memorize pi to 22,514 decimal places and mastered the Icelandic language in seven days.

At the same time, there are downsides to this explosion of talent. Acquired savants are often completely obsessed with their newfound field of interest. Because of the trauma to the brain, there are also serious impacts such as loss of memory, physical pain, isolation, misunderstanding of social norms, and cognitive challenges. Despite that, if given a choice, most acquired savants would not give up their special talent. In a 2012 interview, Padgett said, 'Sometimes I would really like to turn it off, and it won't. But the good far outweighs the bad. I would not give it up for anything.'

But what is the source of this genius that seems to come out of nowhere? Dr Darold Treffert, a respected psychiatrist, offers one theory. With injury to one half of the brain, the other half will become more active to compensate. In a 2013 interview, he explained, 'In the acquired savant with damage to the left hemisphere, there is rewiring to the right hemisphere, there is recruitment of still-intact tissue, and there is release of that dormant potential.' Berit Brogaard, a leading neuroscientist, has a different theory. Her work has shown that when neurons die with brain trauma, they release chemicals which can trigger increased brain activity – which may in turn cause structural changes to the brain, possibly resulting in permanent change.

This seems to suggest that we all are hidden geniuses. Brogaard believes so. In a 2016 interview, she said, 'There's a lot of dormant activity in the brain that could be accessed if we had the means to do so.' She has done studies in which healthy brains are magnetically stimulated and show potential for releasing artistic or mathematical abilities temporarily. She and others are now pursuing research with technology or drugs to help unlock the creative parts of our brains. Treffert also believes that people have more creative potential, but he doesn't necessarily believe technology is the answer. One gentler approach he suggests is accessing different brain circuitry through meditation.

What does this mean for the future? Will we all be geniuses at some point? Will we be able to give our brains a little magnetic zap when we need a new idea? Will a little pill make us more creative? Can we meditate our way to becoming great musicians? Time will tell. Meanwhile, there is the hope we can eventually tap into our creative genius without a blow to the head.

MAKING INFERENCES FROM QUOTES

3 Read the quotes (1–4) from the article on page 37. For each quote, tick ✔ the statement (a–c) that can be inferred.

1 'For me, pi was a shape that you could represent with a number, but I didn't know how to calculate it … All I knew was how to draw it. We're not wired to see things as digits or as numbers. We're wired to see things as shapes.'
   a ☐ Shapes are easier for humans to understand than mathematical formulas.
   b ☐ The speaker wants to know how to calculate pi.
   c ☐ People should learn to draw instead of using numbers.

2 'Sometimes I would really like to turn it off, and it won't. But the good far outweighs the bad. I would not give it up for anything.'
   a ☐ It's possible to turn off his genius ability.
   b ☐ There are some challenges with having a genius ability.
   c ☐ He would like to turn off his genius ability if he could.

3 'In the acquired savant with damage to the left hemisphere, there is rewiring to the right hemisphere, there is recruitment of still-intact tissue, and there is release of that dormant potential.'
   a ☐ A healthy brain does not have dormant potential of creative genius.
   b ☐ Brain injury usually happens on just one side of the brain.
   c ☐ Healthy brain tissue is important in releasing dormant potential of creative genius in a damaged brain.

4 'There's a lot of dormant activity in the brain that could be accessed if we had the means to do so.'
   a ☐ We can access dormant activity in the brain.
   b ☐ We should develop ways to access dormant brain activity.
   c ☐ It will never be possible to access dormant brain activity.

LANGUAGE DEVELOPMENT

UNIT VOCABULARY

4 Complete the sentences using words from the box. You do not need to use all the words.

> procrastinator   suppress   innovative   stimulation   label
> breakthrough   pursue   norms   trigger   notions   sceptical

1 Many psychologists believe that people can experience a creative _____ and suddenly get a burst of ideas after a long period of having none.
2 In those situations, simple things can _____ creativity, such as going for a walk when new ideas emerge.
3 Some people, like Professor Stephen Hawking, are known for having _____ ideas that change the world.
4 Surprisingly, creative thinkers are often _____ , not always trusting data or established beliefs.
5 Research shows that a _____ is often more creative than a colleague who finishes a project early.
6 Groups are often less creative than an individual because when people work together, they usually follow the _____ that have been established over time, which do not easily encourage personal creativity.
7 Because creative children often challenge the rules and lose focus, a teacher may incorrectly _____ a student as 'difficult' or 'unintelligent'.

5 Read the clues and complete the crossword puzzle.

Across
1 To stop a process or reaction (8)
6 A thing that causes something to be more active (11)
8 An accepted standard of behaviour (4)
9 To prove an idea to be true (7)
10 To follow or study (6)
12 To not accept or believe (6)

Down
2 Having doubts (9)
3 Very interesting (10)
4 A belief or idea (6)
5 Able to find new ways to achieve a goal (11)
7 To cause a process or reaction (7)
11 To search for something (4)

EXPERIMENTAL SCIENCE TERMINOLOGY

6 Complete the paragraph using words from the box. You do not need to use all the words.

> control   establishes   conducted   intervention
> implications   contends   subjects

Michael Slepian, a prominent social psychologist, (1)_____ a study in which he looked at how light affects our thinking. He had 79 university students as his research (2)_____ . They had to solve mathematical and verbal problems under either a fluorescent light or a bare light bulb. Those working under the light bulb worked faster and solved more problems. Slepian does not suggest that this (3)_____ a causal link between light bulbs and creativity. Instead, he (4)_____ that – in this case – when one sees a light bulb, a familiar symbol of a bright idea, the brain responds by being more creative. For Slepian, the (5)_____ are clear, 'Our environment can influence our creativity.'

7 Match the words and phrases (1–7) with their definitions (a–g).

1 contend
2 research subjects
3 control group
4 implications
5 conduct a study
6 establish a causal link
7 experimental group

a design and run a research project
b participants in a scientific experiment
c participants who receive treatment, such as a new drug, in a scientific study
d participants who do not receive treatment in a scientific study but are used for comparison
e present an argument based on scientific research
f show a relationship of cause and effect
g conclusions for possible action in the future

8 Complete the text using the words and phrases in the box.

> control group   experimental group
> contend   conducted   research subjects

In 2011, Allan Snyder conducted an academic study with 67 (1)_____.
The study participants in the (2)_____ were given electrical stimulation to two parts of the brain. Snyder and his partner (3)_____ the study by exciting one part of the brain and suppressing another part. Those who were in the (4)_____ did not receive electrical stimulation, although they were told that they did.

The participants were given several puzzles to solve. The study showed that those who received the electrical stimulation were three times better at solving an arithmetic problem than those who didn't receive any. The researchers (5)_____ that people are more creative problem-solvers when they do not rely on established notions but use other parts of their brain.

WRITING

COMPLEX NOUN PHRASES WITH *WHAT*

9 Rewrite the sentences (1–5) so that they contain a complex noun phrase with *what*.

1 In 2003, researchers wanted to know the things that they could do with magnetic brain stimulation to bring out creativity in healthy brains.
   In 2003, researchers wanted to know what they could do with magnetic brain stimulation to bring out creativity in healthy brains.

2 Using research from Dr Brian Miller, the item that Allan Snyder developed was a 'thinking cap'.

3 The thing that this machine does is temporarily imitate brain damage in one part of the brain with electromagnetic zaps.

4 Interestingly, the ability that participants demonstrated when wearing the 'thinking cap' was increased creative and artistic skill.

5 The long-term effect of having the brain manipulated in this way is the one thing that worries some people.

10 Circle the correct phrases to complete the sentences.

1 *What matters most / What matter most* in creative thinking is passion and curiosity.
2 *What do we know / What we know* about creative geniuses is that they are often very independent.
3 It is difficult to know *what that sparks / what sparks* creative ideas.
4 There is still a lot of debate about *what cause / what causes* the changes in a person's brain after a serious injury.
5 Researchers are still trying to learn *what makes / that makes* some people more creative.

USING QUOTATIONS

11 Look at the sentences (1–5) and decide whether they are complete and correct for an academic essay. Tick ✔ the correct box for each sentence.

	complete and correct	not correct
1 According to Dr Robert Epstein, writing in *Psychology Today*, 'The very good news is that, with the right skills, you can boost your own creative output by a factor of ten or more.'		
2 In a 2008 interview with *Scientific American Mind*, Robert Epstein explains, 'When children are very young, they all express creativity, but by the end of the first grade, very few do so. This is because of socialization.'		
3 Robbie Blair, in a 2014 article for the online journal *Lit Reactor*, writes, 'While some high-pressure situations still led to creative outcomes, those instances were rare. High stress and pressure tended to kill creativity.'		
4 Creativity can be cultivated through curiosity, training, and specific exercises designed to foster the imagination, said Bruce Adolphe at the annual Society for Neuroscience meeting in 2013.		
5 According to an article in *The Huffington Post*, 'Creativity is one of the most valued abilities in our society today, particularly within the upper echelons of the workforce.'		

SYNTHESIS

12 Read the essays and tick ✔ the correct box for each description (1–6).

	Essay A	Essay B
1 The author includes quotations.	✔	✔
2 The author uses several different sources.		
3 There is one central idea.		
4 The author includes a personal opinion.		
5 The author cites sources and dates of all quotations.		
6 This is a better essay.		

Essay A

There are many factors that affect creativity, including stress. Current research indicates that stress negatively impacts a person's creativity. Dr Robert Epstein, a well-known psychologist, wrote in a 2009 article in *gradPSYCH* magazine, 'Stress is a creativity killer. When you're in graduate school, there are so many constraints on you. It's detrimental to creative expression.'

This is true not only at university but also in the workplace. Rick Hanson, a neuropsychologist, speaking with *Forbes* magazine in 2012, said, '… when you are chronically stressed, you're less able to be at your best. Particularly when you're talking about a knowledge economy which really places a high premium on creativity.' He notes that constant stress results in a reduced ability to think creatively and to respond quickly to change.

Dr David Rock, Director of the NeuroLeadership Institute and author of *Your Brain at Work*, studies workplace issues. He asserts that creativity is seriously negatively affected when a person is working in a competitive, stressful work environment. In his 2012 article in *Psychology Today*, Rock says, 'Being slightly happy, versus slightly anxious, allows for people to solve more problems and be more creative.'

Essay B

Creativity requires time and reflection. In a *New York Times* article, Jonathan Smallwood from England said, 'Idle mental processing encourages creativity and solutions because imagining your problem when you aren't in it is not the same as reality. Using your imagination means you are, in fact, rethinking the problem in a novel way.' The article goes on to say that several researchers have found that people come up with more ideas when they are not given demanding tasks that keep the mind busy. People need to 'let their mind wander' in order to be more creative. According to an interview with Brigid Schulte in the *Huffington Post*, '… neuroscience is beginning to show that at our most idle, our brains are most open to inspiration and creativity – and history proves that great works of art, philosophy and invention were created during leisure time.'

The implications are clear. We need to slow down and spend time doing nothing. In this way, we will come up with more creative ideas. In a fast-paced culture, all of us need to take time for ourselves and let creativity happen.

GLOSSARY

first grade (US n.) the first year of school
graduate school (US n.) college/university for students who already have a first degree

WRITING TASK

13 Write an explanatory synthesis essay that explores the topic of current trends in accessing creative genius in a healthy brain.

OR

Write an explanatory synthesis essay that explores the topic of current trends in ways to improve creativity.

UNIT 6 CAREERS

READING

IDENTIFYING PURPOSE

1 Scan the article and tick ✔ the correct answer (a–c) to each question.

1 What is the purpose of this article?
a ☐ to convince high school graduates to choose vocational training over college
b ☐ to offer an alternative to a college education
c ☐ to explain why a college degree is not useful

2 Who is most likely to be interested in reading this article?
a ☐ college professors
b ☐ high school academic advisors
c ☐ a student who wants to be a chemical engineer

A real alternative to college

In 2015, 69.2% of high school graduates in the US went to college. Of those, 40% dropped out without getting a degree. College is not the only option, nor is it the right option for everyone. Vocational technical training (vo-tech) offers an alternative, one that is affordable and focused, with a good job placement rate. Vo-tech programmes have traditionally had the reputation of being lower-status 'blue collar' job training courses, but perhaps it is time to rethink this educational category.

For some high school graduates, college is the perfect choice. Those who have done well academically are usually well prepared for the challenges of college, and may have a clear plan for a career that requires a college degree.

But what about those who struggle academically or have no interest in college? What about those who want to work with their hands: repairing engines, building boats, or creating amazing food? There is a lot of pressure from academic advisors and parents to attend college, but perhaps these students would be happier and more successful with vocational training.

In the past, vocational programmes were limited to the trades – plumbing, welding, automotive repair, etc. Today, vo-tech has expanded; in addition to creative programmes like culinary arts or fashion design, they have responded to the need for skilled workers in fast-growing fields. Unlike college, vo-tech programmes offer hands-on work experience, so students are ready for a career as soon as they complete their course of study.

It is hard to dispute the difference in potential earning power between a four-year bachelor's degree and a vocational certificate, but there are other factors to consider. First, the cost of a bachelor's degree is significantly higher than a vocational training certificate, or an associate (two year) degree earned at a community college. As a result, many who finish a bachelor's degree are burdened early in life with huge debt. This difference is clearly illustrated in Figure 1. Second, vo-tech students enter the job market sooner, since programmes take less time than earning a bachelor's degree. Also, job placement for those with technical training is reported to be nearly 100%, while college graduates are finding jobs in their field at a much lower rate, according to a 2012 study at Rutgers University.

Local businesses have benefited from many of the new vocational programmes offered through community colleges. At the Seattle Maritime Academy, students get certification to work in the workboat industry after a nine-month training programme. This is great news for the Washington State Ferry system, where many long-time employees are retiring. In the state of Oregon, an administrator at Columbia Gorge Community College saw a need for technicians to service the wind turbines on the Columbia River, so he started a programme tailored to this industry. Programmes like these are regarded as key to bridging the skills gap.

Most Americans believe that vo-tech programmes are very good at preparing students for work. The results of a survey conducted by the Pew Research Center in 2016, showing the perceived relationship between education and career readiness, are presented in Figure 2. Clearly, vo-tech certificates are seen as better synched to the realities of the job market than either an associate degree or a bachelor's degree.

Despite these perceptions, vo-tech education in the US is not highly regarded. Perhaps it is time to take a lesson from Europe. Though Swiss universities are free, well over half of high school graduates choose vocational programmes funded by some 58,000 Swiss companies. The programmes that are offered in Switzerland reflect the skills that are needed in their labour force. As a result, Switzerland boasts a 3% unemployment rate among young people, compared with 12% in the US. Both businesses and the government are involved in promoting vo-tech programmes, and this educational path is a respected choice.

The value of a vocational technical education is obvious. It offers career opportunities for students who are not interested in or not ready for college. It provides trained workers who are helping to bridge the skills gap in the US workforce. Parents, students and academic advisors need to recognize that there is a real alternative to college – one that can save time and money and lead to a satisfying and successful career.

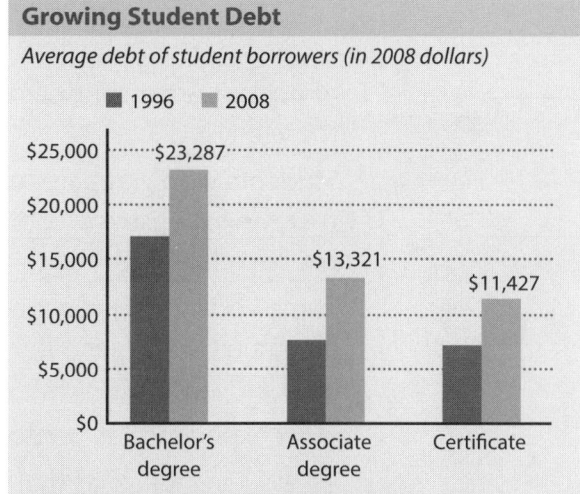

Figure 1. Average debt of student borrowers

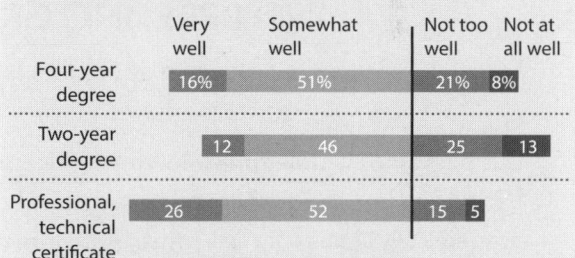

Figure 2. Education and preparation for the workforce

GLOSSARY

college (US n.) university
high school (US n.) secondary school
elementary school (US n.) primary school

READING FOR DETAIL

2 Read the article on pages 46–47. Tick ✔ the correct box for each statement.

	true	false	does not say
1 Almost all Americans earn a college degree these days.			
2 Students who graduate from college think that the expense is worth it because they will get better paying jobs.			
3 Some vocational programmes are offered at community colleges.			
4 One advantage of vo-tech is that students get work experience as part of their education.			
5 To work in industries that are growing rapidly, it will be necessary to have a college degree.			
6 Attitudes toward vocational programmes are similar in Europe and the US.			
7 Businesses financially support vo-tech programmes in Switzerland.			
8 Most students who earn vocational certificates are satisfied with their education.			

INTERPRETING GRAPHICAL INFORMATION

3 Look again at Figures 1–2 from the article on page 47. Tick ✔ the correct answer (a–c) to each question.

Figure 1

1 What is the general trend?
   a ☐ Student debt for college degrees is higher than other educational programmes but debt has increased in all programmes.
   b ☐ Debt for a graduate with a bachelor's degree was nearly $25,000 in 2008.
   c ☐ The cost of education will continue to increase.

2 Based on the information presented, which of these details is correct?
   a ☐ Tuition for a certificate in 2008 was over $11,000.
   b ☐ All graduates who got a bachelor's degree in 2008 owed $23,287.
   c ☐ In 2008, someone earning a bachelor's degree ended up with almost twice as much debt as someone earning vo-tech certification.

Figure 2

3 What is the general trend?
   a ☐ Americans believe certificate programmes are better than college degrees.
   b ☐ Any education will prepare a student for a job.
   c ☐ Americans believe people are better prepared for work with a certificate than with a degree.

4 Based on the information presented, which of these details is correct?
   a ☐ Seventy-eight percent of people surveyed had certificates.
   b ☐ Twenty-six percent of people surveyed thought a certificate programme was good job preparation.
   c ☐ Twenty-nine percent of people surveyed would not choose a four-year college degree.

LANGUAGE DEVELOPMENT

UNIT VOCABULARY

4 Complete the paragraphs using words from the box. You do not need to use all the words.

> assertive   ambiguity   qualified   persistent   boast
> potential   expertise   extend   prospective   chronic

Finding a mentor – or a career guide – is important in any field, and many university graduates seek them out. A mentor should have some (1)_____ in the graduate's field of study and, ideally, also in the specific career the graduate is interested in pursuing. Often, a mentor is a highly experienced person who sees the (2)_____ in a recent graduate and wants to help. The mentor can help a graduate network with other (3)_____ people in the field and may also help the graduate investigate (4)_____ companies.

Corporate mentoring is becoming more common, with 71% of Fortune 500 companies providing mentors to new employees to help them learn their jobs quickly and to act as a resource for questions or concerns. Not all employees need or want a mentor. Those who are more (5)_____ and have no trouble standing up for themselves often feel no need for such a guide. By contrast, a shy employee, who might find it difficult to speak up in meetings or offer ideas, could benefit from mentoring. A mentor can help build confidence and show them the importance of being (6)_____ and bold.

The advantages of good mentoring (7)_____ beyond providing immediate help to new employees, for this year's new employee becomes next year's mentor.

5 Circle the correct words to complete the paragraphs.

Telecommuting might be a good (1)*alternative / illustration / potential* to driving into the office every day for some people. In a recent (2)*dispute / survey / boast*, 85% of telecommuters said they were more productive when working from home. They also said they no longer had (3)*prospective / assertive / chronic* stress from driving in rush hour traffic every day. For businesses, there is a (4)*persistent / qualified / potential* saving when workers telecommute. By one estimate, the savings a company could realize in office space, furniture, supplies and other costs could add up to as much as £8,000 per employee.

Many managers (5)*dispute / extend / diminish* the benefits of telecommuting. Some feel that, without face-to-face contact, the sense of community and common purpose is (6)*extended / diminished / boasted*. Some worry that employees working from home do not do their work. Often, there is no clearly defined list of expectations. It is possible to address this (7)*alternative / ambiguity / illustration*, however, by creating a specific and measurable telecommuting policy that tells the telecommuter – and the company – exactly what is expected.

But telecommuting is not a trend that is going away anytime soon. (8)*Expertise / Potential / Founders* of many start-ups build their businesses with the assumption of telecommuting. In companies like Intel, with 87% of their workforce telecommuting, the business could not function without it.

NOUN + NOUN PHRASES

6 Complete the sentences using phrases from the box. You do not need to use all the phrases.

> entry level   median income   training programmes   earning power
> graduate employment   work–life balance   job market

How to get ahead in your career

1. Get technology skills. You'll have a lot more _____ than those without these skills.

2. Plan for the next step up. At the _____, pay attention to everything around you, especially those above you.

3. Don't forget about your friends and hobbies. To be truly successful, you need a good _____.

4. Keep learning. If your company offers _____, check them out.

5. Keep your CV updated. You never know when the _____ might change and you could need a new job.

7 Match the terms (1–6) with the examples (a–f).

1 median income
2 graduate employment
3 entry level
4 training programme
5 labour force
6 earning power

a as high as £73,000 for a chemical engineer
b University of Cambridge, 89% within three months of graduating
c about 31,500,000 people in the UK
d £36,700 in Bath
e sales rep, starting salary £20,000
f two years for an aviation mechanic

8 Complete the sentences using the phrases in the box.

> participation rate   household income
> vocational training   entry-level   professionals

1 Information technology _____ have a lot of job opportunities these days.
2 In 2014, the City of London had the highest median _____ in the UK, but this is much lower since the recession started.
3 The US labour force _____ has continued to drop every year since 2008, with only 62% of those who can work actually employed.
4 When recruiting people for _____ jobs, many employers prefer those with vocational training because they require less on-the-job training.
5 _____ graduates are often more enthusiastic and have more current knowledge than applicants with academic degrees.

WRITING

ACTIVE OR PASSIVE

9 Look at Figures 1–2 and complete the sentences using the correct active or passive form of the verb in brackets.

1 The labour force participation rate is the US has dropped steadily since 2008. This ten-year decline _____ in Figure 1. (depict)
2 In 2015, millennials replaced baby boomers as the largest generation in the workforce. Figure 2 _____ these results. (illustrate)
3 The labour force participation rate has gone down significantly since 2008. This sharp drop _____ in Figure 1. (demonstrate)

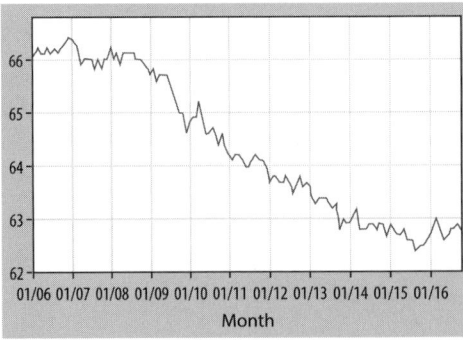

Figure 1. Labour force participation rate in the US

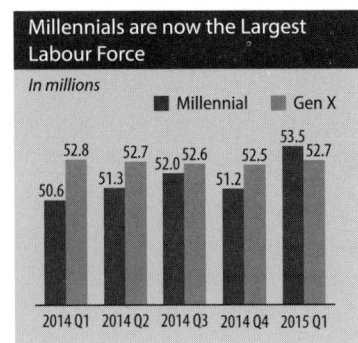

Figure 2. Millennials in the US labour force (in millions)

10 Look at the sentences describing Figures 1–3 in Exercise 9. Rewrite the incorrect sentences. Not all of the sentences are incorrect.

1 Figure 1 is depicted the labour force participation rate over a ten-year period.
   Figure 1 depicts the labour force participation rate over a ten-year period.

2 The engagement of workers with their jobs varies by education type. This difference is showed in Figure 2.

3 A survey of worker engagement reveals that those with a high school diploma are the most engaged with their work. The results is presented in Figure 2.

4 Figure 2 indicates that most workers are not engaged with their work, regardless of the level of education.

5 In the first quarter of 2015, millennials became the largest labour force, replacing baby boomers. This change is represented in Figure 3.

6 After many years of baby boomers being the largest group in the US workforce, they were replaced by millennials in 2015. This shift was appeared in Figure 3.

MAKING A CLAIM

11 Look at the essay task and read the sentences (a–e). Tick ✔ the sentence that would make the best thesis statement for the essay.

Should all companies pay students who work as their interns?
Write an argumentative essay.

a ☐ Students who do paid internships receive more job offers than those in unpaid internships.
b ☐ Internships have real benefits for both the student workers and the businesses, so interns should be paid.
c ☐ Students in accounting and engineering get far more paid internships than students in the humanities, which is not fair.
d ☐ Paid internships are an important step in a career.
e ☐ Paid internships should be the norm for a variety of reasons: legal decisions have indicated interns should be paid; paid interns have better job prospects; businesses gain from the work that interns do.

12 Look at the essay task and match each possible thesis statement (1–4) with the correct criticism of it (a–d).

Millennials are changing jobs much more often than workers in the past. Is this 'job hopping' good or bad for a career? Write an argumentative essay.

_____ 1 Job hopping is not good for building a career for many reasons.
_____ 2 Job hopping is a positive step in a career because the worker gets experience in many places, builds networks, can negotiate better pay, and learns the fastest track to better jobs.
_____ 3 Most of today's college graduates are job hopping, and they believe this helps rather than hurts their career.
_____ 4 Millennials have different ideas about building a career than previous generations.

a The statement doesn't say what the paper is about.
b There are too many details listed in the statement.
c The statement is too broad.
d The statement is factual and cannot be argued.

WRITING TASK

13 Choose a topic from the list and write an argumentative essay with graphical support.

- Should businesses provide mentors for employees starting their career?
- Is telecommuting good or bad for a person's career?
- Is job hopping a positive or negative trend?
- Should companies pay for students to do internships?

UNIT 7 HEALTH SCIENCES

READING

READING FOR MAIN IDEAS

1 Read the letter to a newspaper editor. Tick ✔ the statements that support the author's viewpoint.

a ☐ Parents should have the right not to vaccinate their children.
b ☐ Vaccinations are the responsibility of all people.
c ☐ Those who are elderly or pregnant should get vaccinations.
d ☐ Most childhood diseases can be controlled by vaccinations.
e ☐ The measles outbreak from Disneyland was the fault of parents who didn't vaccinate their children.
f ☐ A very serious situation could result if vaccination rates continue to fall.

MAKING INFERENCES

2 Find the words in bold in the letter, using the context to determine their meaning. Match the words (1–8) with their definitions (a–h).

1 paediatrician
2 immune response
3 immunity
4 suppressed
5 susceptible
6 contain
7 catastrophic
8 pandemic

a causing great damage
b reduced in strength
c spread of disease worldwide
d a doctor who treats children
e protection against disease
f limit
g having little resistance to a disease
h the body's reaction to a disease

VACCINATIONS: A CIVIC RESPONSIBILITY

To the Editor:

As a **paediatrician** who has cared for children for four decades, I must respond to the recent letter by Valerie Redmond, 'Not vaccinating my children is my right.' This 'right' she claims has consequences beyond her own child's health. When Ms Redmond and others in the Anti-Vaccination Movement (known as anti-vaxxers) choose not to vaccinate their children against highly contagious diseases, others in the community suffer. Parents have a responsibility to protect not only their own children, but every other person in proximity to that child.

Since 1924, 100 million cases of serious, contagious diseases have been prevented by vaccinations, as reported in the *New England Journal of Medicine*. The goal of vaccination is the eradication of all vaccine-preventable diseases worldwide. Measles is one of those. It is one of the most highly contagious diseases in the world because its pathogens are easily transmitted in the air when an infected person coughs or sneezes. This is especially true in confined spaces like childcare facilities. Prior to the development of a vaccine in the 1960s, about 2.6 million people around the world died from measles each year, according to the World Health Organization. Since that time, vaccination, which is effective in 97% of children, drove that number down to fewer than 100 cases per year.

In 2015, however, there was a surge in the number of measles cases. One outbreak started in Disneyland in the US, probably from someone who travelled overseas. From this single person, the disease quickly spread to 145 people over seven states and two other countries. Analysis has shown that the outbreak was the direct result of children not being vaccinated. This is one of several outbreaks that year, each one of which could have resulted in an epidemic or even death.

With a vaccine available for such a potentially deadly disease, why would any parent choose not to vaccinate their children? For the answer, we have to go back to 1997, when Dr Andrew Wakefield, a British doctor, published a report claiming that childhood vaccinations contributed to an increase in autism, a brain development disorder. The study was published in a highly regarded medical journal, *The Lancet*, and received a great deal of attention.

Though the results of the study were later proven to be false and the doctor lost his medical licence because of it, the damage was done. The respected reputation of *The Lancet* unfortunately strengthened the idea in people's minds that vaccinations were dangerous. Soon, there were websites dedicated to this notion that parents should not vaccinate their children, eventually resulting in the emergence of the Anti-Vaccination Movement, a loosely organized group of people who have resisted vaccinating their children. Celebrities soon added their voices and continue to do so, despite the overwhelming scientific evidence that vaccinations are safe. The result has been a decrease in immunization rates and an increase in outbreaks of vaccine-preventable diseases, for which the anti-vaxxing movement is directly responsible.

But it is not only the children of the anti-vaxxers who are affected by these outbreaks. Children less than a year old are most vulnerable because they are too young to be vaccinated, but even among healthy people with a good immune response, a small percentage of those who were vaccinated do not respond to the vaccine. As a result, they do not develop the antibodies to protect them against the virus as expected. They too could contract measles from an unvaccinated child. The elderly are another high-risk group because **immunity** becomes weaker as people get older, even among the vaccinated. The effects of the disease are greater with this population because an older person can become much sicker than a younger person. Pregnant women may also be unable to combat pathogens because of a **suppressed immune response** due to pregnancy. Those being treated for certain medical conditions such as cancer are also **susceptible**.

The same argument holds true, by the way, for adults who do not get a flu jab. Measles and the flu are both vaccine-preventable diseases. The old woman beside you on the bus may not be able to fight off an infection when you sneeze. The cancer patient sharing a lift with you has a weakened immune system. And someone's five-month-old baby has no protection at all.

So I ask you, what right is Ms Redmond claiming to have? The right to put vulnerable people at risk of illness or death from a highly contagious and dangerous disease? The only way to **contain** contagious diseases is to have as many people vaccinated as possible. Without mass vaccination, the effects could be **catastrophic**, leading to disease epidemics or even worldwide **pandemics**. While anti-vaxxers may have a legal right not to vaccinate their children, there is a bigger moral issue. They do not have the right to harm others.

Dr Gretchen Klein

CAUSE AND EFFECT ORGANIZATION

3 Read the letter on page 57 again. Put the events in order (1–7) to show a causal chain.

_____ many children are not vaccinated
_____ idea spreads through the internet
_____ more possible outbreaks of diseases that can be prevented
__1__ study about a link between vaccinations and autism is published
_____ children and others exposed to dangerous diseases
_____ parents start the Anti-Vaccination Movement
_____ vaccination rates drop

LANGUAGE DEVELOPMENT

UNIT VOCABULARY

4 Complete the paragraphs using words from the box. You do not need to use all the words.

> proximity   thrive   counter   detection   therapeutic
> grim   eradicated   surge   revolutionize   mild   facilitate

As early as the 1800s, a visit to Davos, Switzerland, was considered (1)_____ for those with tuberculosis (TB) because the high mountain air there was the driest in Europe. For decades, the tiny alpine village was able to (2)_____ as a health resort. Patients got rest, ate nutritious food, and engaged in (3)_____ exercise that was not strenuous enough to hurt their weakened lungs. This treatment was shown to (4)_____ their recovery. By the mid-nineteenth century, there was a (5)_____ in the popularity of fresh-air cures, and more people travelled not only to Davos but also other alpine resorts, like St Moritz.

In the 1950s, that started to change. A vaccine was developed to (6)_____ TB, so the fresh-air cure fell out of favour. Though the vaccination works well, it has not completely (7)_____ the disease yet. The World Health Organization hopes to reach that goal by the year 2035. With a combination of vaccination and early (8)_____ of infection, doctors feel sure TB will soon no longer be a threat to humans.

As for Davos, those who visit now will probably be carrying skis and not tuberculosis – but the air is still dry and pure.

HEALTH SCIENCES   **UNIT 7**

5 Circle the correct words to complete the text.

> Health statistics are ⁽¹⁾*mild / therapeutic / grim* in the world's poorest countries, where millions of people die from preventable diseases every year. In response, the Bill & Melinda Gates Foundation has been sponsoring projects that focus on health research and disease prevention since 2000.
>
> The foundation hopes to see polio ⁽²⁾*revolutionized / bounce back / eradicated* from the world by the end of this decade.
>
> The foundation's work focuses on finding ways to prevent insects from ⁽³⁾*facilitating / transmitting / thriving* diseases like malaria. There is great concern about a drug-resistant type of malaria, which is currently ⁽⁴⁾*confined / eradicated / facilitated* to South East Asia but could spread to other regions if not managed carefully.
>
> The foundation also recognizes that disease prevention can only be successful when the ⁽⁵⁾*cycle / detection / surge* of poverty and poor health, generation after generation, is finally broken.

VERBS AND VERBAL PHRASES FOR CAUSATION

6 Complete the paragraphs using the words and phrases in the box.

> the result of   bring   result   lead
> cause   affect   have an effect   factor

> Many people don't realize the importance of getting enough good sleep. A bad night's sleep might ⁽¹⁾_____ to fatigue or irritability the next day, but over time, it can ⁽²⁾_____ in serious medical conditions like heart disease or diabetes. In addition to overeating and lack of exercise, lack of sleep has been found to be a ⁽³⁾_____ in weight gain and obesity.
>
> Not getting enough sleep can also ⁽⁴⁾_____ on a person's mental health. Studies show that not getting adequate sleep can be a ⁽⁵⁾_____ of depression and anxiety. This is not just a problem for those who cannot sleep, but also for younger people who choose to stay up late rather than going to bed at a sensible time.
>
> Getting too much sleep can also ⁽⁶⁾_____ about dangerous medical conditions. For example, research has indicated that sleeping more than nine hours may ⁽⁷⁾_____ women's heart health. Surprisingly, too much sleep may make people feel more tired than if they had slept only eight hours.
>
> While poor sleep may cause poor health, poor sleep may also be ⁽⁸⁾_____ an underlying medical condition, so people should mention chronic sleeplessness to their doctor.

7 Underline the cause in each sentence (1–7).

1 Many people don't realize how much the <u>use of their smartphone</u> affects the way they feel, both physically and mentally.
2 Leaning the head forwards 60 degrees, as we do when we look at a phone, causes increased stress on the neck.
3 This added weight can lead to a hump in the back, a condition that was once only seen in the elderly but is now seen in teenagers.
4 Another condition, known informally as 'text claw', with cramped fingers and wrist pain, is probably caused by excessive texting.
5 Recently, research has shown that some serious damage to the eyes is the direct result of the blue-violet light of a smartphone.
6 Another study shows that hunching over a phone can negatively influence one's mood as well.
7 The same study indicated that sitting up straight may promote resilience in stressful situations.

VOCABULARY RELATED TO HEALTH AND MEDICINE

8 Complete the sentences using the words in brackets. You will need to change the form of some words.

1 Polio is a highly _____ disease that usually affects children and can lead to permanent paralysis in some cases. (infection)
2 Because polio has no cure, _____ by vaccine is the only way to eradicate it globally. (prevention)
3 Some parents _____ vaccinating their children for polio because they feel it is rare enough not to be a threat. (resistance)
4 Polio vaccines are easily _____ in much of the world, but in remote areas in some developing countries, the vaccine is still not available. (access)
5 Polio is _____ , so it cannot be treated with antibiotics, which only work for bacterial diseases. (virus)
6 Doctors recommend _____ support such as bed rest and fluids while the patient recovers. (therapy)
7 Thanks to vaccinations, this disease has been nearly eradicated; however, a _____ of the polio virus was seen in Congo in 2010, so scientists must start work to develop new vaccines. (mutation)

WRITING

COMMON ERRORS WITH LOGICAL CONNECTORS

9 Circle the correct words and phrases to complete the text.

THE DANGERS OF SUPPLYING DEMAND

A Cashmere, the wonderfully soft wool from special goats, has become more popular as it has become more affordable. Until recently, very few farmers in China raised cashmere goats. However, (1)*because / because of* the global demand for this material, there are ten times as many goats now in the Gobi Desert in Inner Mongolia as there were 60 years ago. Unlike the more gentle cows or sheep, goats are very hard on the rich grassland (2)*because / because of* their sharp hooves cut into the soil, and they destroy the grass by chewing the roots. Desert-like conditions have (3)*resulted from / resulted in* the goat farming; conditions which, in turn, have (4)*resulted from / resulted in* dust storms that have circled the globe.

B Mexico is a top supplier of avocados to the US. As this fruit has become increasingly popular, farmers have cut down their oak and pine trees in order to plant avocado trees. The loss of a great deal of protective habitat for monarch butterflies (5)*is a consequence / as a consequence* of this change. (6)*As a result, / Results from* the number of monarch butterflies that return to Mexico each year has dropped significantly.

C California is the world's largest producer of almonds, another product that has become more and more popular every year. This increased demand is partly (7)*a consequence of / as a consequence* the reputation of almonds as one of most nutritious foods a person could eat. More farmland is now being used to grow almonds (8)*because / as a result*, but almonds require a lot of water. (9)*Because of / Because* California has suffered a drought for over a decade, almond farmers worry that they will not be able to meet the demand for their popular crop.

LOGICAL CONNECTORS

10 Complete the reports using the logical connectors in the boxes.

as a result   due to   because

The damaging effects of earphone use in children

(1)_____ children have shorter ear canals, the use of headphones can be damaging to their ears. Listening to loud music over an extended period can do permanent damage to the hair cells in the ear. (2)_____ , children can suffer permanent hearing loss. (3)_____ an increase in use of headphones, doctors have reported a 30% higher rate of hearing loss in children since the 1990s.

thanks to   so   since

The benefits of 'forest bathing'

Shinrin-yoku, or forest bathing – a Japanese preventive therapy – is now recognized as a valid way to reduce stress, (4)_____ several medical studies. In countries like New Zealand and Japan, doctors actually prescribe walks in the woods to patients instead of medicine, (5)_____ this activity is shown to reduce blood pressure and boost immune function. The government of South Korea wants to encourage the practice of forest bathing, (6)_____ they have invested £100 million in a National Forest Therapy Centre.

consequently   as a result of   since

Death of the Great Barrier Reef

An article in *Outside* magazine recently announced the death of the Great Barrier Reef, (7)_____ the massive bleaching of its colourful coral. Warmer ocean temperatures can cause the coral to lose its symbiotic algae; (8)_____ , it bleaches to a white colour. Some believe that genetic engineering will be required to bring the reef back, (9)_____ the ocean is warming more quickly than the coral can adapt.

WRITING ABOUT CAUSES AND EFFECTS

11 Read the excerpts from previous exercises. Tick ✔ the correct box for each sentence (1–3).

	causes	effects
1 Excerpt 1 mostly analyzes …		
2 Excerpt 2 mostly analyzes …		
3 Excerpt 3 mostly analyzes …		

Excerpt 1

Many people don't realize the importance of getting enough good sleep. A bad night's sleep might lead to fatigue or irritability the next day, but over time, it can result in serious medical conditions like heart disease or diabetes. In addition to overeating and lack of exercise, lack of sleep has been found to be a factor in weight gain and obesity.

Not getting enough sleep can also have an effect on a person's mental health. Studies show that not getting adequate sleep can be a cause of depression and anxiety. This is not just a problem for those who cannot sleep, but also for younger people who choose to stay up late rather than going to bed at a sensible time.

Excerpt 2

Many people don't realize how much the use of their smartphone affects the way they feel, both physically and mentally. Leaning the head forward 60 degrees, as we do when we look at a phone, causes increased stress on the neck. This added weight can lead to a hump in the back, a condition that was once only seen in the elderly but is now seen in teenagers. Another condition, known informally as 'text claw', with cramped fingers and wrist pain, is probably caused by excessive texting. Recently, research has shown that some serious damage to the eyes is the direct result of the blue-violet light of a smartphone. Another study shows that hunching over a phone can negatively influence one's mood as well. The same study indicated that sitting up straight may promote resilience in stressful situations.

Excerpt 3

An article in *Outside* magazine recently announced the death of the Great Barrier Reef as a result of the massive bleaching of its colourful coral. Warmer ocean temperatures can cause the coral to lose its symbiotic algae; consequently, it bleaches to a white colour. Some believe that genetic engineering will be required to bring the reef back since the ocean is warming more quickly than the coral can adapt.

12 Read paragraphs A–C from Exercise 9. Put the events in order to show the causal chains.

Paragraph A
_____ farmers converted to goat farming
_____ worldwide dust storms occur
_____ cashmere became popular
__1__ cashmere was more affordable
_____ goats destroyed grasslands
_____ grasslands became deserts

Paragraph B
_____ fewer butterflies return to Mexico
__1__ avocado demand increases
_____ farmers cut forests down
_____ Monarch butterflies lose protective habitat

Paragraph C
_____ people want more almonds
_____ farmers plant more almond trees
__1__ almonds identified as nutritious

WRITING TASK

13 Use the causal chain describing a drought to write a cause-and-effect essay. Add other effects that you think might result from an extended drought.

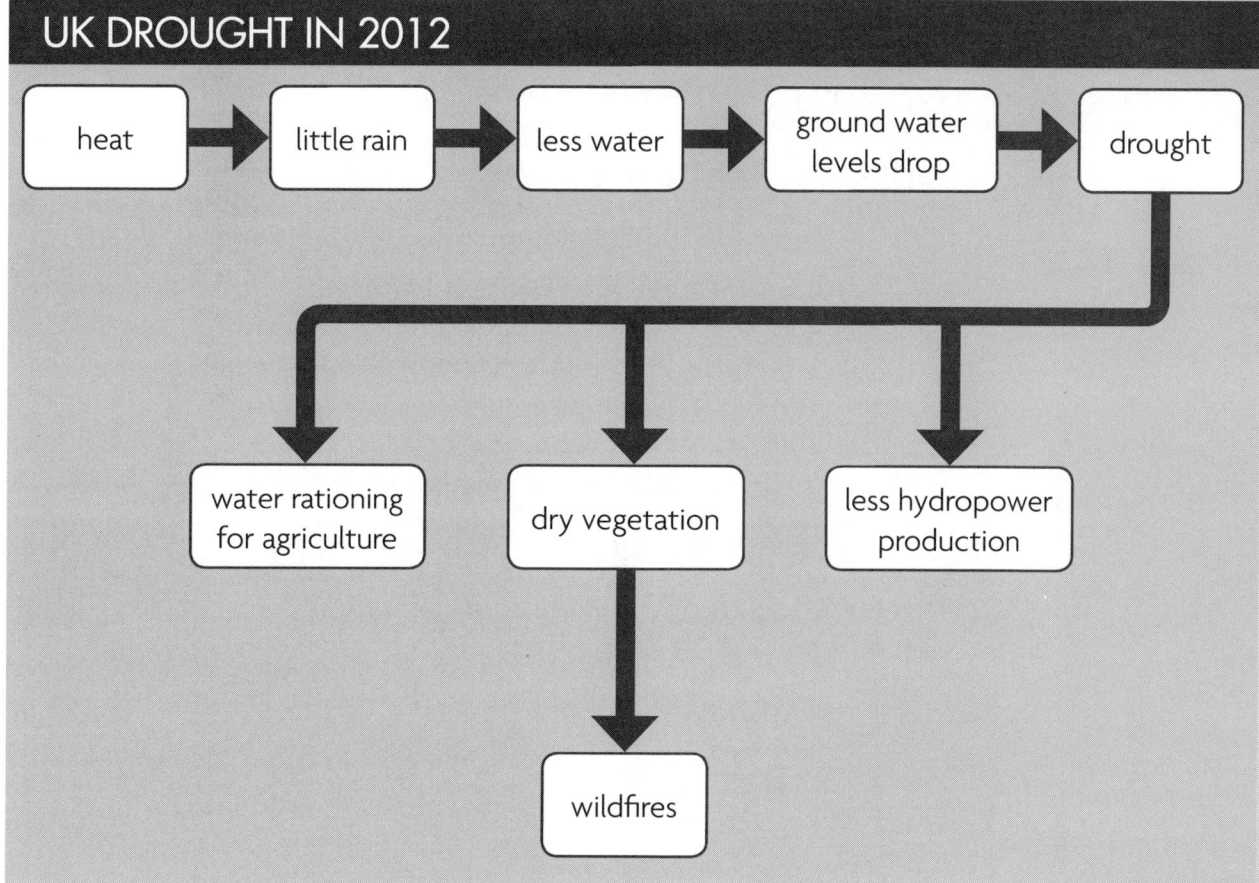

OR

Choose any of the topics from this unit and expand on it to write a cause-and-effect essay.

UNIT 8 COLLABORATION

READING

READING FOR MAIN IDEAS

1 Read the article. Match the topics (1–6) with the paragraphs (A–F).

_____ 1 A design that encourages collaboration
_____ 2 An office design for all workers
_____ 3 The look of the contemporary workspace
_____ 4 In support of privacy
_____ 5 Influences in forming relationships
_____ 6 A need for both collaboration and privacy

READING FOR DETAIL

2 Read the article again. Tick ✔ the correct phrase (a–c) to complete each sentence (1–5).

1 Collaborative workspaces like communal tables and sofas are thought to be
   a ☐ better for team creativity.
   b ☐ more efficient in terms of space.
   c ☐ a sign of energetic activity.

2 Steve Jobs wanted to redesign the Pixar offices because
   a ☐ he wanted everything in one place.
   b ☐ he didn't think people working there needed privacy.
   c ☐ people from different teams weren't interacting.

3 Collaborative spaces may not always be the best work environment because
   a ☐ there can be too many distractions.
   b ☐ people generally do not enjoy working together.
   c ☐ there is not enough time to get the work done.

4 Quiet, private places are important in the workplace because
   a ☐ collaborative spaces are usually too noisy.
   b ☐ some people work better alone.
   c ☐ people can get tired of working with a team all day.

5 The newest office designs address the fact that
   a ☐ many people work from home.
   b ☐ collaboration is no longer important
   c ☐ different workers have different work styles.

Collaboration or solitude?

Collaboration is the norm in most work environments today. Because today's problems are complex and jobs have become more specialized, collaboration is a necessity. How collaboration happens (or doesn't) has affected how workspace design has evolved.

A It is not enough simply to gather a group of like-minded people with diverse skills and tell them to get to work designing this tool or solving that problem. The physical space they occupy while working matters. Today, with collaboration as the goal, large open spaces are the **hallmark** of the modern creative workplace. Instead of individual desks, there are large tables or sofas set up for teams to work together. It is believed that people are more productive and creative in these communal spaces with a steady **hum of activity**. But the big table alone does not lead to successful collaboration. There are other factors at play.

B In the 1940s, a team of psychologists at MIT were looking at how friendships were formed, by studying students who lived in the same building. One would expect that those who had common interests or beliefs would become friends. Instead, those who passed each other casually on a regular basis were the ones who developed friendships. Proximity and crossing paths were the key factors in building relationships. This research eventually influenced ideas about office space and collaboration.

C When Steve Jobs arrived at Pixar as CEO in 1999, the executives, animators and computer scientists were all housed in separate buildings. They didn't cross paths, and, as a result, they didn't really collaborate. Jobs redesigned the office structure so people would be forced to run into others they might not otherwise see. The central space was now a huge high-ceilinged **atrium**, which included mailboxes, a café, and the building's only toilets, as well as a fitness centre. The redesign worked. It led to the random interactions Jobs had hoped for, and those who liked to isolate themselves were forced out of their offices.

D There is no question that collaboration is valuable. Some people **thrive** in a workspace where there is a great deal of energy generated by other creative minds. There is also a better division of labour—the workload tends to be shared among the team. Research shows that a cooperative, supportive workplace may result in more innovative ideas. But while collaboration may be one way to attack a problem, there is evidence that innovators also need to work alone in private, quiet spaces and not constantly be in a **beehive** buzzing with activity. For many, some degree of solitude is a fundamental need.

E Jason Fried, a software developer, speaking in a TED Talk in 2010, **likened** work to sleep by explaining that both demand 'long stretches of uninterrupted time' without distractions in order to really accomplish something. Steve Wozniak, co-founder of Apple, puts it this way: 'Most inventors and engineers I've met are like me … they live in their heads. They're almost like artists. In fact, the very best of them are artists. And artists work best alone … I'm going to give you some advice that might be hard to take. That advice is: Work alone. Not on a committee. Not on a team.' Susan Cain, writer and co-founder of Quiet Revolution, argues that **introverts**, who are often too shy to contribute effectively in collaborative sessions, require privacy in order to be creative.

F Addressing this issue, Barbara Armstrong, a workplace designer, has suggested that in addition to the active open areas, workplaces need to incorporate quiet spaces. In a 2016 article in *Forbes* magazine, she argues that the physical workplace should be diverse, with 'ample space for contemplation, collaboration, and casual collision.' Office designers like Herman Miller are already developing **hybrid** office designs with communal tables as well as private, soundproof rooms for solitary thought.

Companies need to acknowledge the different ways people do their best work. They should provide workspaces where employees can collaborate face to face or work alone, where the **introvert** can work comfortably in an out-of-the-way spot, and the 'people person' can sit down with others. There is no reason that both these employees cannot be productive, creative and happy at their work.

USING CONTEXT CLUES TO UNDERSTAND VOCABULARY

3 Find the words and phrases in bold in the article on page 67, using the context to determine their meaning. Match the words and phrases (1–8) with their definitions (a–h).

1 hallmark
2 hum of activity
3 atrium
4 thrive
5 beehive
6 likened
7 introvert
8 hybrid

a mixed
b a busy workplace
c symbol or feature
d a quiet or shy person
e do well
f low continuous sound
g a large central gathering space
h pointed out the similarities

LANGUAGE DEVELOPMENT

UNIT VOCABULARY

4 Complete the sentences using words and phrases from the box. You do not need to use all the words.

> isolate   gesture   enhance   accomplish   display   detract from
> fundamental   decline   underlie   phenomenon

Decades of research, as well as our personal stories, have confirmed what we know intuitively: we can (1)_____ more together than we can alone. This is true for musicians and actors, designers and engineers, and even teachers and nurses. While many believe that collaboration can have a negative impact on a group's work, studies show that teamwork may actually (2)_____ the quality of what that team produces. Collaboration is especially important for those in fields where their jobs (3)_____ them from colleagues because they mostly work alone, as in teaching or nursing.

Regardless of the field, trust and respect are the personal qualities that (4)_____ most good collaboration. In addition, open communication is (5)_____ to successful teamwork.

It should be recognized, however, that in the last two decades collaboration in the workplace has increased by 50%. In some cases, this has led to a (6)_____ known as 'collaborative overload', a situation that can lead to stress and burnout. It can also (7)_____ the success of a project.

5 Circle the correct words to complete the paragraph.

Wildfires can cover large areas, and fighting them often requires collaboration between several different agencies. In the past, fires on National Forest land in the US were fought (1)*exclusively / apparently* by the US Forest Service firefighters. Today, they work with crews from other agencies and even small local fire departments. Training needs to be (2)*consistent / fundamental* across all agencies, so all firefighters are equally prepared to face any type of danger and to understand all instructions. When there is a fire, leaders have to (3)*differentiate / coordinate* people, supplies, transportation and personnel services very quickly. On the fire line, crews needs to stay focused on their work, because any (4)*display / distraction* could be extremely dangerous. Hotshot crews are elite firefighters. They need to (5)*display / gesture* calmness in the face of danger as an example to others. These coordinated efforts between forestry agencies and firefighting services have paid off. Over the last 20 years, the number of wildfires has steadily and significantly (6)*enhanced / declined*.

LANGUAGE OF HEDGING

6 Tick ✔ the correct box for each statement.

	bold claim	hedged claim
1 People are more likely to be open and share information when they trust others on their team.		
2 There is evidence that women are better collaborators than men because they often have better communication skills.		
3 People will actually expand their skill set by working in a successful collaborative team because they will learn from others.		
4 Introverts are not comfortable sharing their ideas in collaborative work situations.		
5 It appears that groups that work face-to-face are more successful as a team than virtual groups.		
6 Millennials are generally more comfortable than older people when working in a collaborative work environment.		
7 Groups are not effective when one or more of the members is being defensive.		

7 Circle the correct words to complete the hedged statements.

1 It is widely *appeared / assumed / the case* that a brainstorming session will result in a large number of highly creative ideas.
2 However, it may be *thought / the case / evidence* that people are actually less creative when asked to share ideas in a group.
3 In fact, there is *evidence / suggested / the case* that, in a collaborative situation, people tend to mimic what they hear rather than suggest new ideas.
4 It *thinks / appears / is the case* that people are affected by peer pressure, and they want to be seen as friendly and agreeable.
5 It has been *believed / appeared / suggested* that fear of rejection causes many to keep their ideas to themselves rather than share them with the group.
6 It *is evidence / seems / believes* that most people are not even aware that they are doing this.

8 Rewrite the sentences to make hedged claims, using the word or phrase in brackets.

1 In the collaborative economy, sellers are less satisfied than buyers. (somewhat)
   In the collaborative economy, sellers are somewhat less satisfied than buyers.
2 Writers work alone, unlike musicians, for whom collaboration is much more important. (tend to)

3 Team members benefit from training in how to communicate effectively, as well as how to listen without judgement. (may)

4 When leaders in a company don't display cooperative behaviour themselves, their employees resist collaboration also. (are likely to)

5 It's important that managers understand how to get people to collaborate successfully. (generally considered)

6 People who are open to change have more success in collaborative groups. (appear to)

7 The rise in collaboration in the workplace has been rapid, resulting in a challenge for management. (relatively)

WRITING

CONCESSION

9 Circle the correct words and phrases to complete the paragraphs.

COLLABORATION CLASHES IN THE CLASSROOM

(1)*Although / Despite* collaborative learning projects may be good for sharing the workload, it appears that most of the tasks often fall to just one or two students. Additionally, many groups waste a lot of time resolving conflicts or going off topic; (2)*nevertheless, / whereas* according to teachers, students usually get more done in less time when they work in groups. (3)*In spite of / Even though* there may be some friction between group members, a good curriculum based on collaboration will generally teach students the life skills they need to work with others.

THE SHARING ECONOMY

(4)*Despite / While* the new 'sharing economy' has offered many people – such as Uber drivers or Airbnb hosts – an opportunity to work independently, the success of these ventures depends largely on where the freelancer lives. (5)*In spite of / Whereas* the increase in the use of these kinds of services in some areas, the demand for them is apparently not so reliable in other places, making it more or less impossible to make a living. It does seem to be beneficial to a community to have these services available. (6)*On the other hand, / Even though* their presence can negatively impact others, such as licensed taxi drivers and hotel workers.

10 Look at the pairs of sentences (1–6). Tick ✔ the sentence (a–b) in each pair that has the correct sentence construction for the concession language being used.

1 a ☐ Although supermarkets tend to offer lower prices, food cooperatives, or co-ops, are more likely to sell healthier, locally sourced food.
  b ☐ In spite of supermarkets tend to offer lower prices, food cooperatives, or co-ops, are more likely to sell healthier, locally sourced food.

2 a ☐ Despite there is usually a membership fee at a co-op, members generally get special discounts or rebates.
  b ☐ Despite the fact that there is usually a membership fee at a co-op, members generally get special discounts or rebates.

3 a ☐ While customers at a supermarket may be asked for feedback on products, co-op members are often also allowed to give input on how the business itself should be run.
  b ☐ Even if customers at a supermarket may be asked for feedback on specific products, co-op members often are allowed to give input on how the business itself should be run.

4 a ☐ In some areas, food co-ops have grown to the point that they look like supermarkets; nevertheless, they generally still stay true to their mission of providing safe and sustainable products.
  b ☐ In some areas, food co-ops have grown to the point that they look like supermarkets; although they generally still stay true to their mission of providing safe and sustainable products.

5 a ☐ In spite of the fact that supermarkets are often open 24 hours, very few people shop in the hours between midnight and 7 am.
  b ☐ Despite supermarkets are often open 24 hours, very few people shop in the hours between midnight and 7 am.

6 a ☐ Though supermarkets are usually larger and tend to employ more people in a community. The food co-op typically supports the community in other ways, such as buying from local businesses.
  b ☐ Though supermarkets are usually larger and tend to employ more people in a community, a food co-op typically supports the community in other ways, such as buying from local businesses and farmers.

WRITING COUNTER-ARGUMENTS

11 Read the claims and the corresponding counter-arguments in the paragraphs (A–E). Tick ✔ the paragraph that has the best counter-argument to the claim.

☐ **Paragraph A**

Claim: Co-housing is a better housing option.

People tend to believe that having land and a house is the best housing option. Homeowners generally feel that they have relatively more freedom to remodel or to have a garden. Granted, there is often more of a feeling of privacy in one's own home; however, co-housing is a better choice since everyone shares the land and the work.

☐ **Paragraph B**

Claim: Telecommuting does not lead to effective collaboration.

In the modern workplace, many believe that collaboration by telecommuting is effective and efficient. There are usually fewer disruptions when working from home, and it appears that employees are happier in general, which leads to higher retention. On the other hand, it has been suggested that face-to-face collaboration, which often begins with casual interactions in the office hallway, tends to result in more creative ideas and a friendlier workplace. For the best collaboration, telecommuting should be limited.

☐ **Paragraph C**

Claim: Creativity is inhibited by collaboration.

It has been argued that, in business, creativity is more important than knowledge. Creativity generally leads to new ideas and solutions. However, there is evidence that working in groups may limit creativity: Some people, especially introverts, tend to follow the ideas that others put forward instead of sharing their own thoughts. Managers should consider smaller groups so creativity is not inhibited.

☐ **Paragraph D**

Claim: Wikipedia is a useful resource for academic writing.

It is widely believed that Wikipedia is not a good source for academic writing. Generally, non-experts are able to write and edit articles so the information may not be totally reliable. However, there is often a lot of useful information in Wikipedia. When a student does an online search, Wikipedia is usually the first thing that comes up. Wikipedia should be considered an acceptable tool when doing research for academic writing.

☐ **Paragraph E**

Claim: Collaboration between professional and non-professional journalists improves the quality of news reporting.

It is often assumed that accurate news reporting should be done primarily by professional journalists. However, there is evidence that non-professional journalists can be better reporters. They are usually able to report more quickly because they are on the scene and have generally spent more time with the sources. News reports would be more accurate if professional journalists collaborated with non-professional reporters.

12 Read the paragraphs with weak counter-arguments in Exercise 11 again. Match each of the paragraphs with a constructive criticism of it (1–4).

   _C_   1 The counter-argument doesn't disagree with the claim.

   ____   2 The author's claim is not developed.

   ____   3 The counter-argument is not developed.

   ____   4 The supporting reason is weak.

WRITING TASK

13 Read the notes about a design company. Write a report to the company with recommendations for redesigning their office. Include a counter-argument in your report.

Current design
- approximately 150 square feet per person over two floors
- cubicles for 112 employees
- 35 telecommuters
- offices for 4 managers
- one very small kitchen (coffee machine and refrigerator)

Three major areas
- marketing and sales (floor 2)
- product design (floor 1)
- product development (outer building)

Goals
- better collaboration
- more new ideas
- better employee retention

OR

Choose a topic from the list and write an essay in which you make a claim and support it.

- collaborative learning
- collaborative journalism
- co-housing alternatives
- telecommuting and collaboration
- creativity and collaboration

UNIT 9 TECHNOLOGY

READING

PREDICTING CONTENT FROM VISUALS

1 Look at the photographs and tick ✔ the correct answer (a–c) to each question.

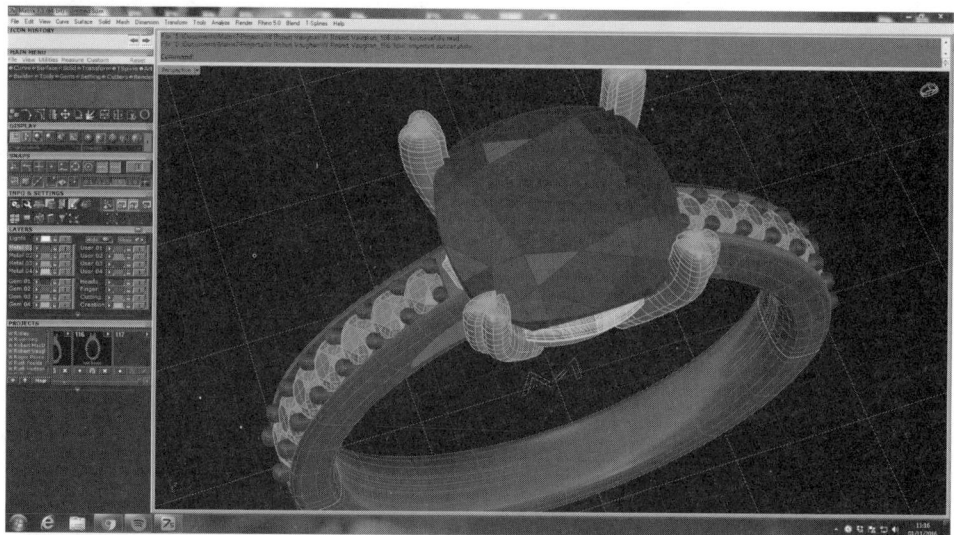

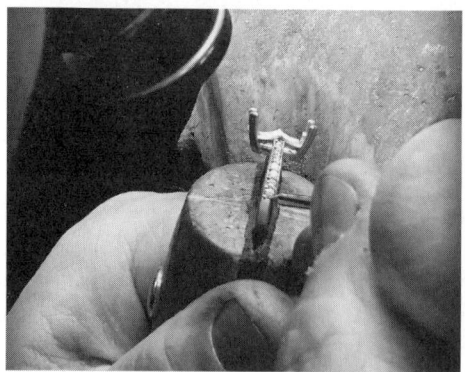

1 How was the jewellery in the photos designed?
   a ☐ with pen and paper
   b ☐ only in the artist's mind
   c ☐ using computer-aided design (CAD)
2 What other industry do you think uses this design process?
   a ☐ fashion
   b ☐ sports
   c ☐ banking

CAD AND 3D PRINTING
Working in partnership to revolutionize product design and manufacturing

THE WORKSHOP

Computer-aided design, or CAD, is one of the most significant **innovations** in IT (information technology) in many years. CAD, as the name suggests, uses computer software to design complex items before they are produced and is used across a wide range of **fields** including architecture, engineering, fashion, shipbuilding and many others.

CAD has a number of benefits, most notably perhaps the fact that it avoids the traditional trial and error approach to product design which typified the 'pen and paper' approach in the days before CAD was so readily available.

In architecture, CAD software can be used to design both detailed floor plans and the whole building. It can also be used to design the more technical aspects such as the required weights of the materials and the volumes.

From civil engineering to mechanical engineering, products can be designed with greater accuracy without wasting time, money and materials on faulty designs. Bridges, roads and whole infrastructure systems can be designed using CAD software.

In shipbuilding, CAD software is used not only for the general structure and accommodation layout of a ship, but can also be used to design on-board shopping centres and swimming pools on cruise ships.

CAD software has also revolutionized the jewellery design process. Jenny Dutson, a Director at The Workshop, a jewellery store which designs and produces **bespoke**, high-quality jewellery, said that CAD software has revolutionized her work as a designer '**inconceivably**'. She added: 'You can build and grow items with the CAD system that you couldn't physically produce at the workbench. You can produce things in a **fraction** of the time and the possibilities are huge so you can make things you'd never have dreamt of before so it gives you more freedom as a designer.'

When the CAD process is finished, however, the product still needs to be produced. This is where another innovation, 3D printing, plays an important role. Although 3D printing has been around in various forms since the 1980s, it is still a relatively new concept for many people.

With 3D printing, products are no longer printed in 2D format on paper but are printed as 3D versions of the image on screen. The process works by cutting each item into tiny slices, resulting in thousands of **cross-section** slices which are printed and placed on top of each other. The slices fuse together to make a complete 3D product. Nowadays products can be printed using plastic, glass, ceramic, metal or even chocolate – in short, anything which can be melted and then sets when it is dry.

Products designed using CAD systems can be printed using 3D printers, which is much faster and cheaper than using traditional methods. This saves time and avoids potentially costly delays in the production of prototypes.

At The Workshop, Jenny's products can be built on 3D printers using precious metals. She explained: 'the process we use is called Precious Metal Sintering. That means you can make a hollow **form** or mould and then that can be printed so you have an item in the hollow form, and both items are metal. This makes the possibilities and the applications endless! You can even scan a 3D item and print out an exact copy.'

But it is not just in the manufacturing world that 3D printers are making an impact. In the medical field, 3D printers are used for education and training. Surgeons can produce **replicas** of a person's organs so that they can practise on the model, for example, a heart or brain, before they carry out complex surgery on a real person. Similarly, medical students can practise surgery without putting patients' lives at risk. However, the items are not just used for practice – replacement limbs, skin, muscles, cells and other body parts have been produced using 3D printing. There will no doubt be many more innovations in the application of 3D technology in the medical field and in many other fields.

Although the exact extent of the impact of CAD software and 3D printing in the future is unknown, it is clear that these two technologies will play an important role across a wide range of fields.

IDENTIFYING MAIN IDEAS

2 Read the article on page 77 and tick ✔ the four main ideas.

a ☐ 3D printing is very expensive.
b ☐ Designing products with CAD is more efficient than designing things on paper.
c ☐ 3D printers can produce products using various materials.
d ☐ CAD can only be used for designing large products.
e ☐ 3D printing can also be used in education.
f ☐ CAD can be used in many fields.

READING FOR DETAIL

3 Read the article again. Tick ✔ the correct box for each statement.

	true	false	does not say
1 Before CAD software, designers had to draw their designs on paper.			
2 CAD software can be used for the visual design but aspects such as weight requirements and volumes must be calculated manually.			
3 Using CAD software means that Jenny can sell her products more cheaply.			
4 Using CAD software allows Jenny to design products that would otherwise be impossible to design.			
5 3D printers have been only become popular in the last five years.			
6 3D printers are more expensive than traditional methods of building prototype products.			
7 3D printers are used to produce organs which can be used for transplants.			

WORKING OUT MEANING FROM CONTEXT

4 Find the words in bold in the article, using the context to determine their meaning. Match the words (1–8) with their definitions (a–h).

1 innovation
2 field
3 bespoke
4 inconceivably
5 fraction
6 cross-section
7 form
8 replica

a an exact copy of something
b in a way that is impossible to imagine or believe
c something that has been cut in half so you can see the inside
d a small part or amount of something
e a hollow, shaped container into which soft or liquid substances are poured, so that when the substance becomes hard it takes the shape of the container
f a new idea, method or development
g tailor-made or made for a particular person
h an area of activity, interest or study

LANGUAGE DEVELOPMENT

UNIT VOCABULARY

5 Complete the sentences using the words in the box.

> aid   superimpose   interpretation   manipulate
> projection   numerous   supplement

1 Using CAD software, you can easily _____ a product's features and design to get the best version of the product.
2 With my new smartphone app, I can _____ information about the place I am visiting onto the view I see in front of me.
3 Innovations in CAD software and 3D printing have _____ advantages for Design Technology lessons. For example, students will be able to print out their designs instead of building them from cardboard.
4 CAD is a great _____ to designers as it gives them much more freedom.
5 Many publishers _____ the content in a textbook with additional online exercises.
6 According to some analysts, the _____ is that the worldwide 3D printing industry will be worth over US $30 billion within the next five years, growing at a rate of over 28% per year.
7 One _____ of the reasons for the success of 3D printing is its wide range of applications in various industries; another is that it has become more popular due to improvements in the technology available.

6 Read the clues and complete the crossword puzzle.

Across
1 To examine carefully (7)
4 Something that is dangerous and likely to cause damage (6)
6 To publicly support or suggest an idea, development, or way of doing something (8)
7 Pleasant, attractive and charming (8)
8 The quality of being new or unusual (7)

Down
1 To be surrounded by something so that you feel completely involved in it (9)
2 Happening at exactly the same time (12)
3 To enthusiastically accept new ideas or methods (7)
5 An area of interest or an area over which a person has control (6)

VERBS TO INTRODUCE EXPERT OPINIONS AND STUDY RESULTS

7 Complete the sentences, using a reporting verb that is suitable for academic writing. Do not use the verbs *say*, *think* or *show*. More than one answer may be possible.

1 Paul Jones _____ , 'Augmented Reality is a novelty now but it will soon become the norm'.
2 One respondent who does not like Virtual Reality _____ , 'Augmented Reality does indeed have many benefits'.
3 Some designers _____ that 3D printing will take over from traditional manufacturing processes within the next 20 years.
4 Researchers _____ that information retention among children is much higher in classrooms which make use of Augmented Reality.
5 Johnson and Malik's (2014) study _____ that the use of CAD and 3D printing can make designing a new apartment block up to ten times faster than using conventional planning methods.

EMPHASIZING OPINIONS WITH CLEFT SENTENCES

8 Put the words in the correct order to make cleft sentences beginning with *It*.

1 3D printers / in the manufacturing world / an impact / it / not just / are making / is / that / .
   It is not just in the manufacturing world that 3D printers are making an impact.

2 the most important / it / the next five years / worldwide / that / for the development of / is / 3D printers / will be / .

3 the jewellery design industry / that / is / has revolutionized / it / CAD software / .

4 has made / it / 3D printing / which / faster and cheaper / product design / is / .

5 the apps / is / are pushing / it / which / for Augmented Reality / the smartphone companies / .

6 the next generation / is / will benefit most / it / from the new technology / who / .

7 that / 3D printers / is / are being used for training and education / in the medical field / very successfully / it / .

WRITING

PARENTHETICAL PHRASES

9 Rewrite the sentences, adding a parenthetical phrase from the box and using appropriate punctuation.

> which is a CAD software application   both in Europe and Asia
> or VR   ~~as the name suggests~~   such as glass, plastic and metal
> perhaps not surprisingly

1 Short Message Service is a way of sending short text messages via mobile phone.
   Short Message Service, as the name suggests, is a way of sending short text messages via mobile phone.

2 The first Virtual Reality headset was designed in the late 1960s.

3 3D printers can use different molten liquids providing the liquid will solidify when dry.

4 Numerous manufacturers have designed innovative products using CAD software.

5 The average person uses less than 30 apps per month but the most popular ones are social networking apps.

6 Rhinoceros is used in many different industries.

USING SEMICOLONS

10 Complete each sentence (1–6) by adding the correct related sentence (a–f) to make one sentence, using a semicolon. You will need to change the capitalization.

1 While it is possible to make jewellery using 3D printing technology, it is still very expensive; nonetheless, we could soon see more bespoke jewellery being offered by high street retailers.

2 According to Forbes, Apple was the eighth largest company in the world on the 2016 Forbes Global 2000_____

3 Architectural Technology studies how buildings look and function_____

4 Shipbuilders are under increasing pressure to produce new concepts fast_____

5 As reliable internet connectivity becomes more widespread in underdeveloped countries, the opportunities for education in remote areas increase_____

6 The possibilities for 3D printers are so endless that many people would like to buy one, but people think they would be too expensive_____

a The drop in prices of smartphones will have a significant impact on this.
b If you have a passion for architecture and are interested in using CAD technology, then this could be the course for you!
c In fact, some 3D printers cost as little as US $100!
d CAD software designers are working on shipbuilding applications to make construction projects more effective.
e ~~Nonetheless, within the next few years, we could see more bespoke jewellery being offered by high street retailers.~~
f However, Chinese banks occupied the top three spots for the world's biggest companies.

FORMAL STYLE IN ACADEMIC WRITING

11 Circle the correct words and phrases to complete the paragraph so that it is sufficiently formal for academic writing.

> You can build (1)*a significant number / loads* of (2)*items / stuff* with the CAD system that you (3)*couldn't / could not* physically produce at the workbench. You can produce (4)*things / goods* in a fraction of the time and the possibilities are huge. You can make products (5)*you would / you'd* never have dreamt of before, which (6)*at the end of the day / ultimately* gives you more freedom as a designer.

12 Find words or phrases in the box with the same meaning as the words and phrases in brackets. Complete the sentences (1–3) using the words and phrases in the box.

> such as   decreased   position   beneficial
> highlighting   considerable   due to

1 There was a _____ (big) increase in sales of 3D printers after a radio report _____ (telling people about) their benefits and the fact that the prices had _____ (gone down).
2 New technology _____ (like) smartphones and VR headsets are always expensive to start with.
3 Studying IT at university can be _____ (good) for your career, _____ (because of) the wide range of opportunities to find a _____ (job) after graduation.

WRITING TASK

13 Write an opinion essay on the topic 'Are new technologies in business always beneficial?' Consider aspects such as the possible impact of new technology on the workforce.

UNIT 10 LANGUAGE

READING

USING YOUR KNOWLEDGE TO PREDICT CONTENT

1 Tick ✔ three factors that are important in learning a second language.
   a ☐ being motivated to learn a second language
   b ☐ being exposed to a second language
   c ☐ knowing a lot of linguistic theories
   d ☐ always speaking in your first language
   e ☐ forming good language-learning habits

READING FOR MAIN IDEAS

2 Read the blog about language learning. Match the headings (1–5) with the paragraphs (A–E).

   _____ 1 Factors that affect our ability to learn a language
   _____ 2 Which one is the most reliable theory?
   _____ 3 Benefits of learning a second language
   _____ 4 Can we learn a foreign language in the same way as we learn our first language?
   _____ 5 How do we learn our first language?

HOW DO WE **LEARN LANGUAGES?**

A Have you ever thought about how you learnt your **mother tongue**? Or how you managed to learn English to such a high level? Do you still forget the third-person 's' (e.g. he read<u>s</u>) every so often? There are a number of theories about how we learn our mother tongue and foreign languages that answer these questions.

Some **linguists** claim that babies and toddlers acquire their L1 (or mother tongue) through imitation and habit formation. This is known as **behaviourism**. For example, if a child says an incomplete sentence, the adult will often reformulate it into a grammatically correct sentence, and the child will (eventually) repeat this.

Other researchers argue that the language produced by toddlers and young children is far too complex for them to have heard everything before they produce it. Noam Chomsky, an influential American linguist, maintains that everyone has an innate ability to learn language. This is known as **innatism**. Chomsky argues that people must be pre-programmed to learn languages and points out that everyone must have a Universal Grammar – a set of principles (like switches) in the brain which are common to all human languages. As a result, we just have to 'set' the switches in our brain to work with the principles of our L1.

Another view of first language **acquisition** is the **interactionist** view. Proponents of this view attach more importance to the environment that the child is in. They argue that language must be simplified so that the child can understand it and, in this way, the child will able to interact with its **caregivers**.

B Unfortunately, there is no definite answer to the question of which **theory** is best, as they have all provided evidence to support their claims so it could be that each theory has some – but perhaps not all – of the answers.

C The theories relating to how we learn a foreign language are similar to those of learning a first language, but the big debate here is whether we learn best in a formal classroom environment or just by acquiring the language.

Again, there is the behaviourist view, which argues that we learn by repeating language and forming habits. On the innatist side, another influential linguist, Stephen Krashen, distinguishes between the effect of formal learning and informal acquisition, and stresses the importance of input which is just above the learner's current level. This is also where you find out why some very advanced language learners often forget the third-person 's': learners acquire the language in a specific order and, although the present simple tense is taught early on, the acquisition of the third-person 's' comes much later. This has also been demonstrated in a number of studies for both L1 and L2 acquisition.

There are also psychological theories which suggest that language acquisition comes from 'noticing' language, while the Interactionist position states that language is acquired by interacting with others.

D In short, then, there are certainly similarities and differences between how people learn their first language and other languages. Perhaps the biggest influence on how quickly people learn a language is time. When they learn their first language, they have months to 'absorb' the language before they speak – but this is not usually the case for a second language learner.

Another aspect which can affect learning is motivation. Children communicate out of need – they want to eat or drink, for example. However, when learning a second language, people may or may not be motivated. Someone learning a language before they move to a country where the language is spoken is likely to be considerably more motivated than a person who has no immediate need to use the language.

E Learning a foreign language can also bring a number of advantages. It is clear that this gives us the opportunity to meet new people and learn about new cultures; however, recent research has also found that speaking two or more languages can delay the onset of mental illnesses such Alzheimer's, a disease which destroys brain cells.

Whatever the factors that affect our ability to acquire language and whether or not we learn in a formal environment, the benefits of learning a second language are considerable.

WORKING OUT MEANING FROM CONTEXT

3 Find the words and phrases in bold in the article, using the context to determine their meaning. Match the words and phrases (1–8) with their definitions (a–h).

_____ 1 mother tongue
_____ 2 linguist
_____ 3 behaviourism
_____ 4 innatism
_____ 5 acquisition
_____ 6 interactionist
_____ 7 caregiver
_____ 8 theory

a someone who studies foreign languages or someone who studies or teaches linguistics
b a theory about how we learn language based on habits and repeating actions
c a theory about how we learn language based on how we communicate with other people
d the first language you learn when you are a baby
e someone who looks after a child, possibly a parent or family member or a nursery teacher
f an idea or explanation for something that is based on known facts but has not yet been proved
g a theory about how we learn language based on abilities that we were born with
h the process of getting, or acquiring, something

READING FOR DETAIL

4 Complete the notes using the phrases in the box.

> which are set to the grammar rules for our L1
> key factors affecting acquisition   second or other (foreign) language
> children need to hear simple language to learn it from others
> a natural ability to learn   in a formal vs informal environment
> imitating people around you   mother tongue

Language learning
- L1 = (1) _____
  - Behaviourism — learn through (2) _____
  - Innatism — Noam Chomsky
    - everyone is born with (3) _____ language
    - Universal Grammar — 'switches' in our brain (4) _____
  - Interactionist approach — (5) _____
- No best theory
- L2 = (6) _____
  - Innatism — Stephen Krashen
    - difference between learning (7) _____
  - need to hear language just above their current level
  - Psychological theories — need to consciously 'notice' language to learn it
- (8) _____ — time and motivation

LANGUAGE DEVELOPMENT

UNIT VOCABULARY

5 Complete the table.

	noun	verb
1	behaviourism, behaviour	behave
2	interaction, interactionist	
3		acquire
4		theorize
5	domination	
6	intervention	
7		predict
8		collaborate

6 Read the clues and find the words in the word search.

1 The study of the origin and history of words: e_____ (9)
2 Having no effect or achieving nothing:
   f_____ (6)
3 Existing or happening in many places and/or among many people:
   w_____ (10)
4 A situation in which something no longer exists: e_____ (10)
5 To make people obey something or do something: e_____ (7)
6 To join a different group and change in order to fit in with that group:
   i_____ (9)
7 Movement from one region to another and often back again:
   m_____ (9)
8 Cause or origin of something: r_____ (4)
9 Special words or expressions used in relation to a particular subject:
   t_____ (11)
10 A form of a language that people speak in a particular part of a country,
   containing some different words and grammar: d_____ (7)

LATIN PREFIXES IN ACADEMIC ENGLISH

7 Complete the sentences using the words in the box.

> pre-school   interact   disestablish
> pre-pay   collaborate   postwar   interpretation

1 If you _____ an organization or group, you take power away from it.
2 In some countries, _____ children are offered free nursery places.
3 I often work together with a colleague from another university on projects; we _____ very well.
4 You need to _____ for the language course.
5 We often talk about the time after the Second World War as the _____ years.
6 Just because we see things differently does not mean one of us is wrong; we simply have a different _____ of the situation.
7 It is good to see children who speak different languages playing together; even though they don't share the same language, they still manage to _____ well with each other.

HIGHLIGHTING SUPPORTING DETAILS

8 Match the sentence halves. Underline the phrases which introduce the supporting details.

____c____ 1 In Spain, some languages,
_____ 2 Some aspects of language are acquired very late,
_____ 3 As exemplified by the fact that we use the Russian words 'sputnik' and 'cosmonaut',
_____ 4 It is estimated that there are around 350 million native speakers of English but between 1.5 and 2 billion people who speak English globally;
_____ 5 As demonstrated by the poor test results,

a we can see that foreign words are integrated into English.
b the students had still not mastered the use of the Present Perfect.
c <u>such as</u> Catalan, were prohibited under Franco.
d specifically the third-person 's' in English.
e that is, there are far more non-native speakers than native speakers.

WRITING

REDUCED RELATIVE CLAUSES

9 Rewrite the sentences. Replace the relative clause with a reduced relative clause using a gerund or past participle.

1 The theories which relate to how we learn a foreign language are similar to those of learning a first language.
   The theories relating to how we learn a foreign language are similar to those of learning a first language.

2 Other researchers claim that the language which is produced by toddlers and young children is far too complex for them to have heard everything before they produce it.

3 When words are introduced into other languages, they sometimes change their spelling, such as *sugar*, which is derived from the Arabic word *sukkar*.

4 Researchers who support Noam Chomsky's theory of Universal Grammar also believe this exists in L2 learners.

5 Some English words, which are entering the French language via social media, still do not have French equivalents.

6 Linguists who are concerned about the prevalence of English claim that this will lead to the loss of local languages.

7 More and more academics who are taught in English are publishing in the English language.

8 People who are learning a new language may find it helpful to repeat sentences they hear to practise the intonation.

PRESENTING RESEARCH FINDINGS

10 Circle the correct words to complete the sentences.

1 Research *suggests / is suggesting* that interaction is a key aspect of language learning.
2 The study *was revealing / revealed* some interesting findings related to short-term memory and language acquisition.
3 The findings *will indicate / indicate* that children need to read every day in the school holidays to maintain their vocabulary level.
4 While Alameri's 2014 study *resulted / is resulting* in different outcomes, this does not necessarily discredit the claims in Gutierrez's 1985 paper.

AVOIDING OVERGENERALIZATIONS

11 Rewrite the sentences using the correct form of the words and phrases in brackets.

1 Spanish will become the most widely spoken language in the world in the next 50 years. (be highly unlikely)
   It is highly unlikely that Spanish will become the most widely spoken language in the world in the next 50 years.

2 It was thought that the minority language Ayapaneco would become extinct, but now speakers are teaching the language to others so it will not die out. (be highly unlikely)

3 Foreign words are adopted into languages when there is no exact translation for the foreign word. (to be likely)

4 To reduce the number of foreign words in a language, some academic institutions invent new words in their language. (might)

5 Arabic and Chinese will become the most popular foreign languages after English in the next few years. (may well)

6 In 100 years' time, there will be no minority languages anywhere in the world, because everyone will be speaking the dominant language in their area. (be possible)

7 The widespread use of English means that all young people are effectively bilingual in English and their native language. (may have the effect)

_____

_____

12 Rewrite the statements to make them less generalized, using the word or phrase in brackets. You will need to add extra words for some statements.

1 Gifted linguists can learn to speak many languages fluently. (few)
A few gifted linguists can learn to speak many languages fluently.

2 Students learning a foreign language use online games and computer programmes to practise. (significant proportion)

_____

3 Linguists believe that everyone possesses a Universal Grammar, which enables them to learn their L1. (some)

_____

4 Linguists believe that we also have a Universal Grammar for our L2. (number)

_____

5 Morpheme studies show that all people learn languages in the same order. (nearly)

_____

6 People in Scandinavia speak English fluently. (many)

_____

WRITING TASK

13 Write a problem–solution essay with the title 'The influence of new technologies on the growing importance of English is having a major impact on minority languages, which are rapidly dying out. What can be done to prevent the extinction of minority languages?'

ACKNOWLEDGEMENTS

The authors and publishers acknowledge the following sources of copyright material and are grateful for the permissions granted. While every effort has been made, it has not always been possible to identify the sources of all the material used, or to trace all copyright holders. If any omissions are brought to our notice, we will be happy to include the appropriate acknowledgements on reprinting and in the next update to the digital edition, as applicable.

Text acknowledgements
Graph on p. 47 adapted from 'Is College Worth It?'. Pew Research Center, Washington, DC (May, 2011) http://www.pewsocialtrends.org/2011/05/15/chapter-3-public-views-and-experiences/; Graph on p. 47 adapted from 'Key findings about the American workforce and the changing job market'. Pew Research Center, Washington, DC (October, 2016) http://www.pewresearch.org/fact-tank/2016/10/06/key-findings-about-the-american-workforce-and-the-changing-job-market/; Graph on p. 52 from 'Labor Force Statistics from the Current Population Survey. U.S. Bureau of Labor Statistics; Graph on p. 52 (millennials) adapted from 'Millennials Surpass Gen Xers as the Largest Generation in U.S. Labor Force'. Pew Research Center, Washington, DC (May, 2015) http://www.pewresearch.org/fact-tank/2015/05/11/millennials-surpass-gen-xers-as-the-largest-generation-in-u-s-labor-force/ft_15-05-11_millennialslargest/.

Photo acknowledgements
Key: T = Top, B = Below, BL = Below Left, BR = Below Right, BG = Background.

p. 5 (T): Michael Kline/Moment Editorial/Getty Images; p. 5 (BG): Mike Kline (notkalvin)/Moment/Getty Images; p. 13: Luigi Masella/EyeEm/Getty Images; p. 15: Martchan/iStock Editorial/Getty Images Plus/Getty Images; p. 21: Image Source/Getty Images; p. 24: Paul Bradbury/OJO Images/Getty Images; p. 29: Jeff Greenberg/Universal Images Group/Getty Images; p. 37 (BL): Lionel Bonaventure/AFP/Getty Images; p. 37 (BR): Bettmann/Getty Images; p. 55, p. 87 (B): Hero Images/Getty Images; p. 57 (T): JGI/Tom Grill/Blend Images/Getty Images; p. 57 (B): KidStock/Blend Images/Getty Images; p. 67: JohnnyGreig/E+/Getty Images; p. 87 (T): David Sacks/DigitalVision/Getty Images; p. 90 (T): Chris Tobin/DigitalVision/Getty Images; p. 90 (B): Caiaimage/Chris Ryan/OJO+/Getty Images.

Cover Photography by STRINGER/AFP/Getty Images.

We are grateful to the company for permission to use copyrighted logo and the commissioned photos on pp. 76, 77: Jenny Dutson/The Workshop.

Corpus
Development of this publication has made use of the Cambridge English Corpus (CEC). The CEC is a multi-billion word computer database of contemporary spoken and written English. It includes British English, American English, and other varieties of English. It also includes the Cambridge Learner Corpus, developed in collaboration with the University of Cambridge ESOL Examinations. Cambridge University Press has built up the CEC to provide evidence about language use that helps to produce better language teaching materials

Cambridge Dictionaries
Cambridge dictionaries are the world's most widely used dictionaries for learners of English. The dictionaries are available in print and online at dictionary.cambridge.org. Copyright © Cambridge University Press, reproduced with permission.

URLS
The publisher has used its best endeavours to ensure that the URLs for external websites referred to in this book are correct and active at the time of going to press. However, the publisher has no responsibility for the websites and can make no guarantee that a site will remain live or that the content is or will remain appropriate.

Typeset by emc design ltd.

UNL⊘CK

LISTENING & SPEAKING SKILLS 5

Laurie Frazier and Carolyn Westbrook

CONTENTS

UNIT 1	Conservation	4
UNIT 2	Design	12
UNIT 3	Privacy	20
UNIT 4	Business	28
UNIT 5	Psychology	36
UNIT 6	Careers	44
UNIT 7	Health sciences	52
UNIT 8	Collaboration	60
UNIT 9	Technology	68
UNIT 10	Language	76
Audio scripts		84
Acknowledgements		104

UNIT 1 CONSERVATION

LISTENING

LISTENING TO INTRODUCTIONS

1 🔊 1.1 Listen to the introduction to a radio interview. Circle the correct words and phrases to complete the sentences.

1 International Dark Sky Week was established by *an astronomer / (a secondary school student) / the government*.
2 International Dark Sky Week is a *city / national / global* event.
3 The goal of International Dark Sky Week is to draw attention to light pollution and ways to *combat / accumulate / document* it.
4 Light pollution is the brightening of the sky caused by *natural light / man-made light / starlight*.
5 Light pollution affects *eight / eighteen / eighty* percent of the world's population.

CONSERVATION   UNIT 1

IDENTIFYING RHETORICAL QUESTIONS

2 🔊 1.2 Listen to the radio interview. Are the questions asked (1–8) real or rhetorical? Tick ✔ the correct box for each question.

	real	rhetorical
1 What is International Dark Sky Week?		✔
2 Its goal?		
3 Why are you interested in light pollution here on Earth?		
4 Are there other negative effects of light pollution?		
5 But aren't lights necessary for safety, especially in cities?		
6 And what about environmental problems caused by light pollution?		
7 How's that?		
8 Why not do what we can to combat it?		

LISTENING FOR DETAIL

3 🔊 1.2 Listen again and circle the correct words to complete the sentences.

1 Astronomers study *light pollution /(stars and deep space)/ city lights*.
2 Fewer than *80 / 100 / 200* years ago, everyone could see the night sky and Milky Way.
3 According to the guest speaker, increased lighting does not reduce *costs / crime / wildlife* in cities.
4 Artificial light can make it difficult for people to *study / sleep / travel*.
5 Light pollution causes many animals to be more vulnerable to *hunger / heat / predators*.
6 Baby sea turtles hatch from their eggs *on beaches / in the ocean / near hotels*.
7 Baby sea turtles rely on *street lights / moonlight / starlight* to find their way to the ocean.
8 In North America, up to one *thousand / million / billion* birds crash into artificially lit buildings every year.

LANGUAGE DEVELOPMENT

UNIT VOCABULARY

4 Complete the crossword puzzle.

Across
4 To happen or make something happen more quickly (10)
6 Easy to hurt or attack (10)
7 More than enough (adj.) (8)

Down
1 Money that a business receives regularly (7)
2 Having never happened in the past (13)
3 To give something as part of a total amount (8)
5 Able to succeed (6)

CONSERVATION — UNIT 1

5 Complete the sentences using the words in the box.

> divert combat accumulate shameful
> ~~yield~~ intensive nutrients conversion

1 The farmer acquired more land, which increased his annual ____yield____ by 25%.
2 Fruits and vegetables contain key _____ for good health.
3 The _____ of beaches into holiday resort areas has resulted in an increase in light pollution.
4 The topsoil in this area has eroded largely because of _____ farming practices.
5 One way to _____ light pollution is simply to turn off lights when they are not in use.
6 The amount of energy that is wasted in this country is _____ . We all should work harder to reduce our energy use.
7 Do you think the government should _____ money from the military to environmental conservation?
8 Because of the way the river bends right here, rubbish and other waste tends to _____ along this side. The city really needs to clean this up.

PARALLEL STRUCTURE IN COMPARISONS

6 Look at the sentences (1–6) and decide whether they contain parallel structure or not. Tick ✔ the correct box for each sentence.

	parallel	not parallel
1 Urban areas produce more light pollution than rural areas.		✔
2 The Milky Way is much harder to see at night now than it was in the past.		
3 Street lights waste more energy than household lights do.		
4 The pollution caused by bright lights is greater than dim lights.		
5 Sea turtles that hatch near hotels are at greater risk than those that hatch in dark areas.		
6 Migratory birds are more vulnerable than local bird populations.		

7 Put the words in the correct order to make sentences.

1 results in / than / intensive farming / erosion / rotating crops / less / does / .
   <u>Rotating crops results in less erosion than intensive farming does.</u>

2 environmental damage / crop farming / has caused / cattle farming / has / more / than / .

3 uses / water / other industries / than / do / agriculture / more / .

4 profitable / our neighbour's / more / is / than / our farm / farm / .

5 those / wheat yields in China / greater / in India / are / than / .

6 almonds / does / than / California / more / produces / any other state / .

THE LANGUAGE OF ARGUMENT – BLAME AND RESPONSIBILITY

8 Complete the sentences using phrases from the box. You do not need to use all the phrases.

> dropped the ball   falling on her sword   bear the responsibility
> step up   held to the same standard   ~~point fingers~~
> take the blame   credited with   ducking responsibility

1 It is easy to _____**point fingers**_____ at agriculture for wasting water and energy, but we all _____ for conservation.
2 Secondary school student Jennifer Barlow is _____ _____ establishing International Dark Sky Week.
3 Many say the automotive industry has _____ when it comes to producing more fuel-efficient cars.
4 Major polluters need to _____ and _____ for the damage they cause to the environment.
5 Many resort hotels are no longer _____ for endangering wildlife with their bright lights. They are working with environmentalists and educating their guests in order to help the wildlife follow their natural patterns.

CONSERVATION — UNIT 1

PRONUNCIATION

INTONATION OF COMPLETE AND INCOMPLETE IDEAS

9 🔊 1.3 Listen to the sentences (1–8) from the interview in Exercise 2. Write *C* if the sentence is complete and *I* if it is incomplete.

1 It was first established in 2003 by secondary school student Jennifer Barlow. ___I___
2 Large cities obviously produce the most light pollution. _____
3 Here to tell us more is astronomer Melanie Turow. _____
4 Astronomers study stars and deep space. _____
5 But light pollution actually affects all of us. _____
6 Most of us who live in the city probably never think about it. _____
7 Baby sea turtles hatch from their eggs on beaches. _____
8 And light pollution is totally preventable. _____

SPEAKING

CHALLENGING OTHER POINTS OF VIEW

10 Match the expressions (1–16) to the patterns (a–d).

a direct challenge of a position
b concession + challenge of a position
c dismissal of point as not important/irrelevant
d statement of conditions for agreement

___a___ 1 That doesn't follow.
_____ 2 I suppose, but …
_____ 3 And what happens if …
_____ 4 That's not necessarily true.
_____ 5 That's irrelevant.
_____ 6 That may be true, but …
_____ 7 That would be fine, except …
_____ 8 On the contrary, …
_____ 9 I would agree with you if …
_____ 10 That's not the point.
_____ 11 I agree up to a point.
_____ 12 Actually, …
_____ 13 That might be the case if …
_____ 14 You have a point. However, …
_____ 15 How can you say that?
_____ 16 Not necessarily.

11 Complete the conversation using the words and phrases in the box.

> actually   but   that's not the point   how can you say that
> I suppose   what happens if   not necessarily

Mike: So what do you think of the new light I installed outside our house?

Ava: Well, it looks nice, I guess, but is it really necessary?

Mike: I think so. I wanted a bright light on the front of the house for safety, to see what's going on and keep criminals away.

Ava: (1) _____I suppose_____ it's important to be able to see, (2) _____ that light is too bright.

Mike: So, you think I should take it down? (3) _____ we come home late at night and can't see where we're going? We could trip over something and fall down. And it'll keep the house safe while we're away.

Ava: (4) _____ . Lights help criminals see, too. And lights that are too bright can actually reduce your ability to see. Most crimes happen during the daytime anyway. But (5) _____ . I don't like it because bright lights are wasteful, and they cause light pollution.

Mike: Light pollution? (6) _____ ? It's only one light. How can that cause pollution?

Ava: (7) _____ , any bright light contributes to light pollution. You could put in a dimmer light, and make sure to point it downward. That way, you're saving energy, and you're limiting the light you put into the sky.

SPEAKING TASK

12 Imagine you are going to present an argument about zoos, answering the following question:

Are zoos beneficial or harmful to animals?

1 Choose a position.

Arguments in favour of zoos
- Zoos educate the public and encourage human interaction with animals. This motivates people to protect animals.
- Zoos protect endangered species by providing them with a safe place to live where they are not vulnerable to starvation, habitat loss, or predators.
- Good zoos provide habitats where animals are well cared for and have plenty of space.

Arguments against zoos
- Animals in zoos suffer from stress and boredom. Some zoos neglect, harm, and kill their animals.
- Breeding in zoos leads to overpopulation of animals. These animals are often sold to circuses, hunters, or for food.
- Animals sometimes escape zoos, harming people and other animals.

2 Make notes to support your argument.
- Your point of view
- Supporting points for your position
- A challenge to an opposing point of view

3 If you can work with another student or your teacher, present your argument.
- Be sure that comparisons you make are parallel.
- Use expressions of blame and responsibility where appropriate.
- Listen to other points of view and challenge them with appropriate expressions.

UNIT 2 DESIGN

LISTENING

PREDICTING CONTENT USING VISUALS

1 🔊 2.1 Look at the photographs and tick ✔ the correct word or phrase (a–c) to complete each sentence. Then listen to the student presentation about industrial design and check your answers.

1 The presentation will be about a …
   a ☐ product.
   b ☐ company.
   c ☐ designer.

2 The presentation will be about …
   a ☐ sinks.
   b ☐ taps.
   c ☐ hand dryers.

3 The presentation will focus on how the design …
   a ☐ improved.
   b ☐ was manufactured.
   c ☐ failed.

LISTENING FOR MAIN IDEAS

2 🔊 2.1 Listen again and circle the correct words or phrases to complete the sentences.

1. For most of the twentieth century, hand dryer technology *became more expensive / didn't change / dramatically improved*.
2. The Xlerator was developed by a team of retired *scientists / designers / businesspeople*.
3. Old hand dryers wasted ninety percent of the *money / energy / work* that went into them.
4. New hand dryers are much *louder / faster / cheaper* than old hand dryers.
5. People generally prefer to use *their clothes / hand dryers / paper towels* to dry their hands.
6. Hand dryers are *better than / worse than / as bad as* paper towels for the environment.

USING A GRAPHIC ORGANIZER TO CAPTURE DETAILS

3 🔊 2.1 Listen again and complete the table using the words and phrases in the box.

> 12 seconds   slow, warm air   fast, unheated air   2006   ~~1949~~
> fast, warm air   about 60 seconds   2001   10 seconds

name	World Dryer	Xlerator	Airblade
year developed	(1) 1949	(4)	(7)
time to dry hands	(2)	(5)	(8)
method of drying	(3)	(6)	(9)

LANGUAGE DEVELOPMENT

UNIT VOCABULARY

4 Match the words and phrases (1–8) with their definitions (a–h).

1 assembly
2 foundation
3 mass production
4 shift
5 backlash
6 circumvent
7 phenomenon
8 finite

a to avoid something by going around it
b a strong negative reaction
c the thing on which other things are based
d the process of putting parts together to create one thing
e something happening that is noticeable because it is new or unusual
f to change position or focus
g the process of producing large numbers of one thing in a factory
h limited; set and fixed

5 Complete the sentences using the words in the box.

> resent   obstacle   scenario   customize
> downside   devised   subsequent   drastically

1 My new phone is fast and powerful. The _____ is, it's too big to fit in the front pocket of my jeans.
2 The Xlerator is available in chrome, white, or black, or you can _____ it with a colour of your choice.
3 We _____ reduced the price of our product hoping the low prices would increase sales.
4 In the best-case _____, our sales would increase by 30%.
5 The oil crisis of the 1970s had an impact on the automotive industry. _____ car models became more fuel efficient.
6 I _____ the fact that products are designed for obsolescence. It's wrong to make people buy the same things again and again.
7 Our marketing department has _____ a very clever campaign that we're sure will increase sales.
8 The primary _____ to improving the design of our product is finding a lighter weight material that is as strong as the original.

USING CAUSE-AND-EFFECT PHRASES

6 Match the sentence halves.

___e___ 1 By creating faster hand dryers,
_____ 2 3D printing has the potential to drastically change manufacturing,
_____ 3 Recent models of hand dryers include pans to catch dripping water,
_____ 4 3D printing may result in a huge increase in rubbish
_____ 5 By creating new organs from a patient's own cells,

a disrupting the supply chain.
b 3D printing lowers the risk of rejection by the patient's body.
c reducing the water that ends up on the floors of public toilets.
d by making it too easy for people to replace items.
e manufacturers encourage people to choose them instead of paper towels.

EXPRESSING AN EFFECT

7 Rewrite each sentence, replacing the non-defining relative clause with a phrase expressing the effect.

1 People tend to use paper towels instead of hand dryers, which produces a lot of unnecessary rubbish.
People tend to use paper towels instead of hand dryers, producing a lot of unnecessary rubbish.

2 Germs remain on wet hands, which results in the spread of illness to others. _____

3 Some hand dryers can blow germs off hands and into the surrounding air, which makes them unsuitable for hospitals.
_____

4 Planning for a product's obsolescence involves using cheaper materials, which means lower costs for consumers.
_____

5 Many high-tech products are designed to work for only a short time, which encourages constant innovation.
_____

6 Consumers often can't find replacement parts for their devices, which prevents them from making repairs.
_____

DEGREE EXPRESSIONS

8 Put the words in the correct order to make sentences using degree expressions.

1 too / designer fashions / expensive / to afford / for most people / are / .
___
___

2 enough / the high price / of this jacket / to justify / the quality / isn't / good / .
___
___

3 low / to encourage / to buy / the prices / more than they need / of fast fashion / are / enough / consumers / .
___
___

4 badly made / for more than / is / most fast fashion / one season / too / to wear / .
___
___

5 quickly / to meet / didn't reach / the new dresses / the demands of shoppers / enough / shops / .
___
___

PRONUNCIATION

WORD STRESS

9 🔊 2.2 Listen to the words and phrases and underline the stressed syllable.

1 mass pro<u>duc</u>tion
2 drastically
3 manufacturer
4 downsides
5 inefficient
6 technology
7 devised
8 horse race
9 subsequent

SPEAKING

ACKNOWLEDGING OTHER ARGUMENTS

10 For each expression (1–7), tick ✔ the box (a–c) that describes the pattern.

	a position A + concession expression + position B	b concession introduction + position A + position B	c concession introduction + position A + concession expression + position B
1 There are two sides to the situation: …			
2 On the one hand, … on the other hand, …			
3 … Having said that, …			
4 Many people think that …, some others say that …			
5 There are two ways of looking at …			
6 Granted, …, but …			
7 … That said, …			

11 Complete the sentences using the words and phrases in the box.

> granted   that said   on the one hand
> there are two ways of looking at   on the other hand

1 _____ , electric cars use less fuel, which saves money. _____ , the replacement batteries can be very expensive.

2 Electric cars are cheaper to maintain than petrol-powered cars. _____ , many owners will need to make an initial investment to install a charging station at home.

3 _____ , electric cars don't run out of petrol, but they do need to be recharged frequently.

4 _____ electric cars: either they help the environment by reducing fuel consumption and emissions, or they hurt it by producing more pollution in the manufacturing process.

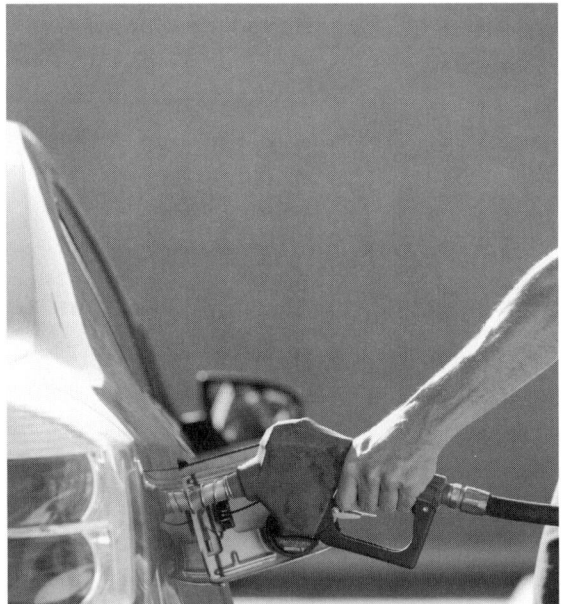

SPEAKING TASK

12 Imagine you are going to give a presentation about a product or a technological advance, discussing the pros and cons of its use.

1. Choose a product or a technological advance.
   - 3D printers
   - Cell phones
   - Video games
   - Electric hand dryers
   - Other: _____

2. Make notes to support your presentation.
   - Introduce and describe the product or technological advance.
   - Explain the pros of its use.
   - Explain the cons of its use.
   - Conclude with your own opinion.

3. If you can work with another student or your teacher, give your presentation.
   - Use cause and effect phrases and degree expressions where appropriate.
   - Acknowledge other arguments.
   - Use correct word and syllable stress.

UNIT 3 PRIVACY

LISTENING

LISTENING FOR MAIN IDEAS

1 🔊 3.1 Listen to the podcast and circle the correct words to complete the sentences.

1 The main topic of the podcast is *data privacy / tech innovations / computer passwords*.
2 Most students in the research study failed to *create a strong password / update the software / read the privacy policy* before signing up for a social app.
3 It is important to turn on automatic *software / password / webcam* updates.
4 Most people create passwords that are too *predictable / random / long*.
5 According to the speaker, it isn't necessary to share your *photos / location / username* with most apps.
6 The speaker suggests covering your laptop's *webcam / login screen / keyboard*.

LISTENING FOR DETAIL

2 🔊 3.1 Listen again and complete the notes using the words and phrases in the box.

> firstborn child   locks   tracked   symbols   tradeoffs
> identity   record   oversharing   74   social media
> manager   long   6   hackers   turn off

main ideas	details
privacy (1)_____ for using digital technology	• location (2)_____ • credit card no. in the cloud • pop-up ads • (3)_____ theft • future = ?
most people don't know what they're sharing/ agreeing to	• Example: research study • (4)_____ % students didn't read privacy policy • agreed to give up (5)_____
five ways to protect privacy:	
1 turn on auto software updates	• protects against (6)_____ & identity thieves
2 use screen (7)_____	• prevent stranger access to personal info • (8)_____ + characters; not easy to guess
3 make unbreakable passwords	• strong password = (9)_____ & random • list of words + no.s, (10)_____, caps; story to remember • use password (11)_____ app
4 stop (12)_____	• delete phone no., email & address from (13)_____ • (14)_____ location sharing
5 cover laptop webcam	• hackers secretly (15)_____ computer activity • use tape or a sticky note

LISTENING FOR OPINIONS

3 🔊 **3.2** Listen to the sentences and tick ✔ the correct box for each sentence.

	fact	opinion	neither
1 If you're like me, you love your personal digital technology.			
2 In their experiment, seventy-four percent of the students who joined didn't even read the privacy policy.			
3 We have to be better at protecting our personal data.			
4 So today I'd like to share with you five simple ways you can protect your privacy.			
5 Probably the most critical thing you can do to counter threats to your privacy is to keep your operating system and software up to date.			
6 Your screen lock should be at least six characters long.			
7 You can turn off location sharing in your phone's settings.			

LANGUAGE DEVELOPMENT

ACADEMIC VOCABULARY

4 Complete the crossword puzzle.

Across
4 Able to make you believe something is true or right (10)
5 The way that something has been done in the past that therefore shows that it is the correct way (9)

Down
1 Allowed according to law, or reasonable and acceptable (10)
2 A collection of weapons (7)
3 To defend against or respond to (7)
4 To force or pressure (6)
6 To find the origin of something (5)

5 Complete the sentences using the words and phrases in the box.

> trade-off   targeted   caught up with   encryption
> informed   expertise   creepy   track

1 I was sick last week, and I haven't _____ my work. I'm still behind.
2 Many consumers don't realize that companies _____ their online activity.
3 I know it's important to stay _____ about a site's privacy policy, but the documents are usually so long that I just click 'I accept' without reading them.
4 I have excellent _____ software on my computer, so I'm sure my files are safe from hackers.
5 Their new ad campaign is _____ at teenagers.
6 I find it _____ that companies follow us online to collect and sell our personal data.
7 The _____ for having a strong password is having to remember it!
8 My computer science professor has _____ in data analytics and programming.

SUBJECT–VERB AGREEMENT WITH QUANTIFIERS

6 Complete the sentences using the correct form of the verbs in brackets.

1 About 46 percent of the global population _____ access to the Internet. (have)
2 The majority of people _____ passwords that are too easy to guess. (create)
3 About 70 percent of millennials _____ mobile apps to do their banking. (use)
4 Most of my free time _____ into using social media. (go)
5 Some recent research _____ that people are becoming more concerned about online privacy. (show)
6 A number of students _____ their friends during class, even though they know phones are forbidden. (text)
7 Many said they were paying attention, but few _____ able to recall the homework assignment. (be)
8 A quarter of the test _____ based on the lecture material. (be)

COLLOCATIONS

7 Match the sentence halves from the box with sentences 1–6.

> surf the web.   disable cookies.   search engine.
> I'm on a secure network.   I clear my cookies.   search terms.

1 Google is the most popular _____.

2 It usually gives me the best results when I enter _____.

3 When I get home from school, I like to _____.

4 I avoid doing my banking or shopping online unless _____.

5 After shopping online, I always log out and _____.

6 When I'm using a public computer, I prefer to _____.

8 Complete the paragraph using phrases from the box. You do not need to use all the phrases.

> break the law   combatting crimes   committing crimes
> obey the law   enforce the laws   law enforcement   law-abiding

As people become more active online, they become more vulnerable to cybercrimes. For this reason, (1)_____ needs to put more time and effort into (2)_____ such as security breaches, identity theft and online fraud. Most internet users are (3)_____ citizens who act responsibly and never (4)_____. Investigators and technical experts need to work together to protect them. They should monitor online activity and (5)_____ that exist for honest business. And when they find cyber thieves at work, they should prosecute them for (6)_____ online, just as they would any other type of thief.

PRONUNCIATION

SENTENCE STRESS

9 🔊 3.3 Listen and underline the stressed words in each sentence.
1 There are tradeoffs for these modern conveniences.
2 You want to buy those shoes online?
3 Then your credit card number is in the cloud.
4 Set your software to update automatically.
5 Use screen locks on all of your devices.
6 A strong password should be long and random.
7 If you need to, add some numbers, symbols or capital letters.
8 You can turn off location sharing in your phone's settings.

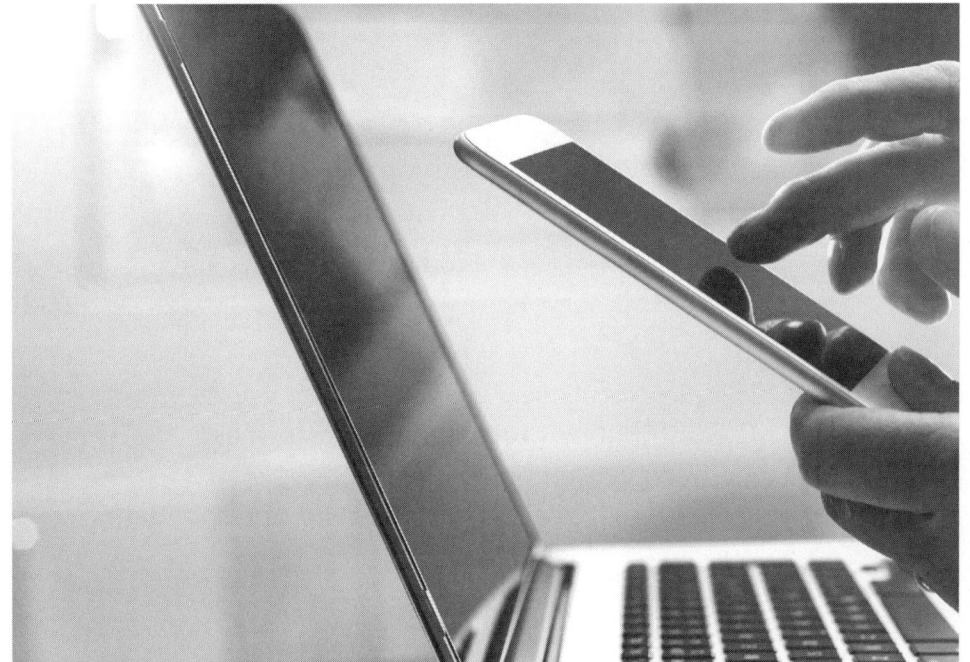

SPEAKING

EXPLAINING DATA FROM GRAPHICS

10 Match the sentence halves to explain the graphic data.

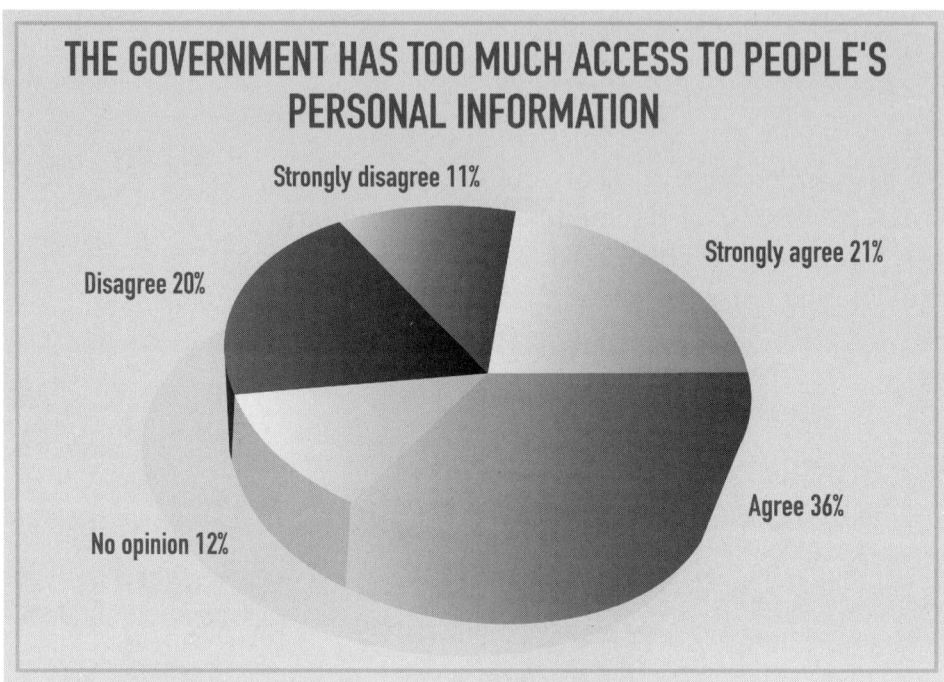

_____ 1 This pie chart shows
_____ 2 The distribution of responses is somewhat
_____ 3 The survey results indicate most people
_____ 4 It can be seen that almost one-third of respondents
_____ 5 We can conclude that

a disagree with the statement.
b uneven.
c the results of our survey question about government access to people's personal information.
d agree that the government has too much access to our personal information.
e there is a disagreement about this issue.

11 Complete the description of a graphic using the words in the box.

> majority   survey   demonstrates
> follows   results   respondents

This graph shows the (1)_____ of our first (2)_____ question. The (3)_____ of people feel that consumers have lost control over how personal information is collected and used by companies. Only nine percent of (4)_____ feel they have a lot of control over how their information is collected and used. This (5)_____ that people are concerned about loss of privacy. It (6)_____ that these concerns should be addressed openly in the privacy policies of online retailers.

SPEAKING TASK

12 Imagine you are going to give a presentation on the data collected from a survey about online privacy.

1 Review the graph.

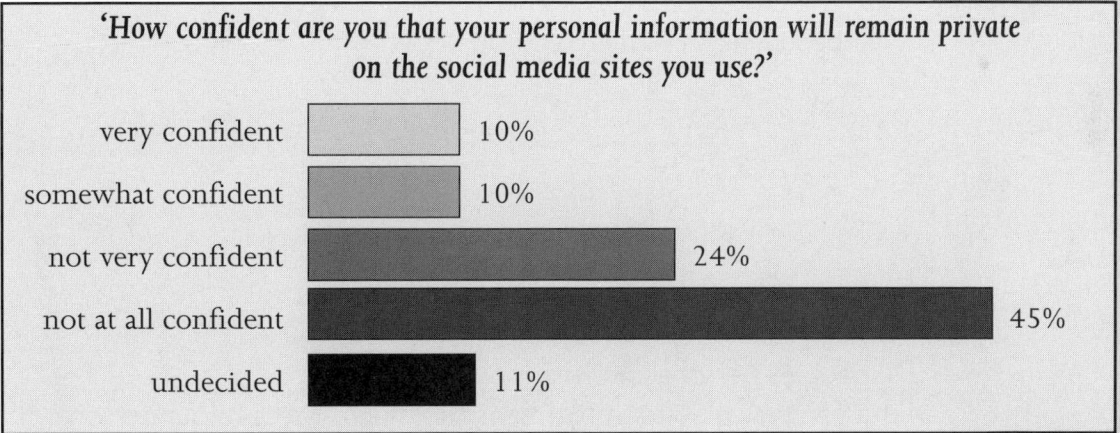

2 Prepare talking points to explain the survey results.
- Introduce the survey question.
- Explain the results of the survey.
- Present the conclusions you have drawn from the data.

3 If you can work with another student or your teacher, give your presentation.
- Use language for presenting data from graphics and drawing conclusions.
- Be aware of subject–verb agreement with quantifiers.
- Use appropriate sentence stress and question intonation.

UNIT 4 BUSINESS

LISTENING

LISTENING FOR MAIN IDEAS

1 🔊 4.1 Listen to the classroom discussion. Tick ✔ the correct box for each sentence.

	true	false
1 Corporations can be for-profit or non-profit.		
2 The goal of traditional for-profit corporations is to benefit society.		
3 A benefit corporation is a non-profit organization.		
4 Benefit corporations are certified by the government.		
5 The professor believes there are advantages to becoming a certified B corporation.		

2 🔊 4.1 Listen again and circle the correct words to complete the sentences.

1 A corporation is considered a legal *person / business / organization*.
2 Milton Friedman considered increasing profits to be the only *legal / social / professional* responsibility of business.
3 Benefit corporations were established in *1987 / 2007 / 1970*.
4 The non-profit group B Lab provides B corps with *oversight / partnerships / employees*.
5 The number of B corps has *increased / stayed the same / decreased*.
6 B corp certification can help a company to *follow its mission / put profits first / create advertising*.
7 B corp certification assures consumers that a company *is profitable / uses buzzwords / is trustworthy*.
8 Many young people want to work for a company with *talented employees / a social mission / lower salaries*.

LISTENING FOR DEFINITIONS

3 🔊 4.2 Listen and complete the sentences with the words and phrases being defined. Use no more than three words in each answer.

1 In other words, a _____ is an organization that is legally separate from the people who own and run it.
2 Most corporations, however, are businesses, whose goal is to _____ – to make money.
3 Maximizing profits is great for _____ – that is, the investors who make money through owning shares in the company.
4 But that can come at a cost to other _____ – meaning those who are affected by the actions of a corporation.
5 A _____ is a for-profit corporation that is required by law to achieve a positive impact – on its workers, the community, society, and the environment – in addition to making a profit.

LANGUAGE DEVELOPMENT

UNIT VOCABULARY

4 Match the words (1–8) with their definitions (a–h).

1 transaction
2 aggregator
3 dump
4 facilitate
5 funding
6 mission
7 oversight
8 status

a supervision over, management of
b to make easier
c a tool that collects and organizes information
d money for a particular purpose
e an activity that involves the movement of money
f official position
g to drop, without caring where
h goal or purpose, especially of an organization

5 Complete the sentences using the words in the box.

> scope   elaborate   fabulous   buzzwords
> effectively   overload   overview   concisely

1 Since my co-worker went on holiday, I have _____ done her job and mine.
2 I am suffering from information _____ after attending new employee orientation. I have a lot to learn in a short time.
3 My new company has an _____ procedure for every process. I don't know if I'll ever remember them all!
4 I wanted to impress the interviewer with my communication skills, so I spoke as clearly and _____ as possible.
5 He did a _____ job on his presentation. Everyone was impressed.
6 He provided an _____ of the topic before explaining the details.
7 She uses a lot of _____ on her CV, but her experience isn't very impressive.
8 The _____ of this project is too large for one person to handle. I'll need to get some help.

COMPLEX COMPARISONS AND CONTRASTS

6 Complete the sentences using *even*, *let alone*, or *not to mention*.

1 It seems that some corporations don't care much about their own employees, _____ people in the community.
2 The exam was so difficult that _____ the top students in the class had a hard time finishing it.
3 This non-profit is offering me a job with a good salary and great benefits, _____ a social mission that I believe in.
4 She had changed so much that _____ her own family didn't recognize her.
5 I don't have enough money saved to buy a new bike, _____ a car.
6 It takes time and effort, _____ dedication, to succeed at university.

ACADEMIC ALTERNATIVES

7 Complete the crossword puzzle using academic alternatives to the words in the clues.

Across
3 Kind; type (5)
5 Very large (adj.) (7)
6 Business (7)

Down
1 To stop using (7)
2 Main (7)
4 To sort (v.) (4)
7 To come out (v.) (6)
8 A sign (n.) (5)

8 Complete the sentences using words from the box. You do not need to use all the words.

> emerged   trace   massive   venture
> option   breed   primary   sifted   abandon

1 Her latest _____ is her most successful yet. Profits doubled last year.
2 The _____ goal of most traditional corporations is to increase profits.
3 We haven't been able to raise enough money, so we have to _____ our plans to expand the business.
4 My company just announced _____ layoffs. Nearly one-third of the employees are going to lose their jobs.
5 I have the _____ of staying with the company if I relocate to a different city. My other choice is to find a new job.
6 During the 1980s, Ben & Jerry's _____ as a leader in the ice cream industry.
7 We _____ through a lot of CVs before finding any good candidates for the new position.

PRONUNCIATION

THOUGHT GROUPS

9 🔊 4.3 Listen to the sentences and underline the final word in each thought group.

1 A corporation is considered a 'legal <u>person</u>' because it can enter into <u>contracts</u>, loan and borrow <u>money</u>, hire <u>employees</u>, buy <u>property</u>, and pay <u>taxes</u> – just like a <u>person</u>.
2 The mission of non-profit corporations, of course, is to provide some kind of social good.
3 In fact, since the 1970s, most for-profit corporations have followed the thinking of economist Milton Friedman, who considered increasing profits to be the 'only social responsibility of business'.
4 Maximizing profits is great for shareholders, that is, the investors who make money through owning shares in the company.
5 So, in 2007, a new type of corporation, called a 'benefit corporation', or B corp, was created to help business owners do just that.
6 Some companies claim to be socially or environmentally conscious and use buzzwords like 'green' or 'natural' in their advertising, but B corp certification assures customers that a company is living up to its promises.

SPEAKING

MISSION STATEMENTS

10 Read the mission statements of four organizations and match each part (1–12) to the information it provides (a–c).

a Why the organization exists
b Who it serves
c How it serves them

Doctors Without Borders
___a___ 1 We help people worldwide, where the need is greatest,
_____ 2 delivering emergency medical aid
_____ 3 to people affected by conflict, epidemics, disasters, or exclusion from health care.

The New York Times
_____ 7 To enhance
_____ 8 society
_____ 9 by creating, collecting and distributing high-quality news and information.

Seventh Generation
_____ 4 To inspire a consumer revolution
_____ 5 that nurtures the health of
_____ 6 the next seven generations.

The Lending Club
_____ 10 To transform the banking system to make credit more affordable and investing more rewarding.
_____ 11 The company's technology platform enables it to deliver innovative solutions
_____ 12 to borrowers and investors.

MAKING A PITCH

11 Read the pitch and decide whether each of the elements of a good pitch is present. Write *P* for present and *M* for missing.

> In 2006, we had a dream of building a world where business is dedicated not just to making a profit, but to making the world a better place. Since then, we have fostered thousands of companies around the globe who share our dream, and today, you have the opportunity to join us by supporting B Lab. At B Lab our mission is to serve 'a global movement of people using business as a force for good'. Our vision is that 'one day all companies compete not only to be the best in the world, but the best for the world'. We are making this dream a reality by creating a global community of Certified B Corporations™ and verifying that they meet the highest standards for benefitting society and the environment. We help B Corporations align their missions to the needs of society and manage their impact through our unique assessments and analysis. At the same time, we are measuring our impact by tracking the growing number of socially responsible businesses inspired to join our movement. So what are you waiting for? Now is the time. Seize this opportunity and 'be the change' for a better world. Support B Lab.

1 Give a clear, concise mission statement.   _____
2 Include a story to illustrate the need for your venture.   _____
3 Explain how you will achieve your goals.   _____
4 Offer a measure of success.   _____
5 Use imagery.   _____
6 End with a strong statement of support for your venture and yourself.   _____

SPEAKING TASK

12 Imagine you were the founder of a major organization before it became successful. You are going to make a pitch to get your peer-to-peer business or non-profit organization started.

1 Choose a peer-to-peer business or a non-profit organization.
- Airbnb
- Uber
- Etsy
- eBay
- Lending Club
- Kiva
- Doctors Without Borders
- Other: _____

2 Prepare talking points for a pitch to get funding.
- Give a clear, concise mission statement.
- Include a story to illustrate the need for your venture.
- Explain how you will achieve your goals.
- Offer a measure of success.
- Appeal to listeners' emotions.
- End with a strong statement of support for your venture and yourself.

3 If you can work with another student or your teacher, make your pitch.
- Use academic alternatives to high-frequency vocabulary.
- Use figurative language when possible.
- Pause at the end of thought groups.

UNIT 5 PSYCHOLOGY

LISTENING

LISTENING FOR MAIN IDEAS

1 🔊 5.1 Listen to the lecture and circle the correct words and phrases to complete the sentences.

1 Attention Deficit Hyperactivity Disorder (ADHD) is a *brain / personality / mood* disorder that affects children.
2 The main symptoms of ADHD are inattention, hyperactivity, and *impulsivity / anxiety / headaches*.
3 Hyperactivity describes children who have trouble *focusing on a task / have difficulty sitting still / act before thinking about the results of their actions*.
4 To diagnose ADHD, the symptoms must be present before the child is *six / twelve / seventeen* and must impair the child in at least two settings.
5 Treatment options for ADHD include medication and *psychotherapy / behaviour therapy / shock therapy*.
6 About *one-third / a half / two-thirds* of children with ADHD use prescription medication.
7 Side effects of ADHD medication can include sleep difficulties, headaches, stomach aches, and loss of *concentration / memory / appetite*.
8 The number of children diagnosed with ADHD is *rising / falling / staying the same*.

LISTENING FOR GENERALIZATIONS AND SUMMARIES

2 🔊 **5.1** Listen again and match the signals (1–5) to the generalizations and summaries (a–e).

_____ 1 In short,
_____ 2 In general,
_____ 3 So, what causes ADHD? The bottom line is
_____ 4 Overall,
_____ 5 To sum up,

a ADHD is not a simple condition to diagnose.
b while we don't know the exact cause of ADHD, we do know that ADHD can be successfully treated.
c children with ADHD have problems with inattention, hyperactivity, and impulsivity. But some may have trouble with only one of these behaviours, and the symptoms can change over time.
d it's clear that ADHD is a problem that requires further research to help us better understand its causes and develop more effective prevention and treatment options.
e we don't know for sure.

LISTENING FOR DEPENDENCY RELATIONSHIPS

3 🔊 **5.2** Listen again to part of the lecture. Complete the transcript with the words and phrases you hear that signal partial dependency relationships.

> So, what causes ADHD? The bottom line is we don't know for sure. There are a number of possible ⁽¹⁾_____factors_____ . One ⁽²⁾_____ is genetics. ADHD can run in families. Environment is another possible ⁽³⁾_____ .
> Some speculate that exposure to drugs, alcohol, or smoking during pregnancy can ⁽⁴⁾_____ ADHD in the baby, just as exposure to environmental toxins – such as lead paint – can ⁽⁵⁾_____ it in children. Another ⁽⁶⁾_____ is premature birth, which can negatively ⁽⁷⁾_____ brain development.

4 🔊 5.3 Listen again to part of the lecture. Complete the transcript with the words and phrases you hear that signal dependency relationships.

> So what's causing this increase? Some believe there is no increase. We just have a name now for something that has always existed. Others speculate that ADHD is ⁽¹⁾_____ poor sleeping habits or exposure to electronics, or ⁽²⁾_____ not enough time spent playing outdoors. Others worry that the increase ⁽³⁾_____ the pressure put on kids from schools and parents to improve academic performance. ⁽⁴⁾_____ , doctors may be too quick to diagnose ADHD and prescribe medications to people who don't need it.

LANGUAGE DEVELOPMENT

UNIT VOCABULARY

5 Complete the crossword puzzle.

Across
3 To worsen (11)
4 Skilled; able to do things well (9)
6 To establish one's location (6)
7 A way in which something can be used (11)

Down
1 A signal; something that causes a response (3)
2 A place or structure that is easy to recognize (8)
3 Specialized (14)
5 Behaviour that aims to control others (9)

6 Complete the sentences using the words in the box.

> reconstruct   intriguing   impair   exposure
> speculate   approachable   definitively   navigate

1 Psychologists _____ that premature birth may lead to ADHD in children.
2 _____ to bright light helps some sufferers of Seasonal Affective Disorder, a form of depression that occurs in the winter months when there is less daylight.
3 The results of this study are _____ . I am interested in reading the follow-up studies.
4 My psychology professor is not very _____ . I'm nervous about visiting him during his office hours.
5 I had trouble following the lecture. I tried to _____ the key points later, but my notes didn't make sense!
6 Scientists are unable to say _____ what causes ADHD.
7 My spatial memory isn't very good. I usually rely on GPS to _____ while I'm driving.
8 ADHD can _____ a student's ability to perform well in tests.

NOUN CLAUSES WITH *WH-* WORDS AND *IF/WHETHER*

7 Rewrite each pair of sentences (1–5) as one sentence, changing the question into a noun clause. For some sentences, more than one answer is possible.

1 What causes ADHD? We aren't sure exactly.
   We aren't sure exactly what causes ADHD. /
   We aren't sure what exactly causes ADHD.

2 Is ADHD overdiagnosed? Researchers are trying to find out.
   _____

3 Who are most likely to be diagnosed with ADHD? It's the youngest students in a class.
   _____

4 How well do London taxi drivers find their way around? It's amazing.
   _____

5 Did the hippocampi of London taxi drivers grow larger? Researchers took MRI images to find out.
   _____

ACADEMIC WORD FAMILIES

8 Complete the table with the correct noun forms.

	adjective	noun
1	approachable	approachability
2	aggressive	
3	attractive	
4	competent	
5	thoughtful	
6	dominant	
7	likeable	

9 Complete the sentences using words from the table in Exercise 8. You do not need to use all the words.

1 She is well-known for her _____ . Her patients are comfortable going to her with questions.
2 Children with ADHD are more likely to show signs of _____ , such as bullying or fighting with others.
3 This exam is designed to measure our writing _____ . If you pass, you aren't required to take any more writing courses.
4 How _____ of you to write a personal thank-you note.
5 My new flatmate is very _____ . I think we're going to get along well.
6 He is definitely the _____ one in that relationship. He's always telling her what to do.

PRONUNCIATION

EMPHASIS WITHIN THOUGHT GROUPS

10 🔊 **5.4** Listen to the sentences (1–8) taken from the lecture. Underline the emphasized words in each thought group.

1. So what is ADHD?
2. First of all, | inattention.
3. Children with inattention are easily distracted | and make careless mistakes | in schoolwork | or other activities.
4. They also may have difficulty | following instructions | and staying organized.
5. Hyperactivity | describes children | who are overly active.
6. Hyperactive children | seem to be constantly 'on the move', | have difficulty sitting still, | and may talk too much.
7. Finally, | impulsivity describes someone | who acts | before thinking about the result | of their actions.
8. Impulsive children | often have difficulty waiting their turn | and may interrupt others.

SPEAKING

TALKING ABOUT RESEARCH

11 Put the talking points (a–k) in the correct place in the table according to their category.

a Can people judge how likeable, competent, trustworthy, and aggressive a person is based on a photo of the person's face?
b Both studies focused on first impressions; however, the first study focused on a variety of traits, while the second focused only on attractiveness.
c People make judgments about others in just a tenth of a second and these judgments are consistent with people who have unlimited time to make them.
d It will help us understand attractiveness.
e How do people decide if they would want to date someone based on their picture compared to meeting them in person?
f Different preferences suggest we each make different judgments about what constitutes a 'good catch'.
g It will help us understand how quickly first impressions are made.
h Being able to decide if you can trust someone quickly was important for evolution.
i Both studies show that first impressions are made very quickly and those impressions last.
j People's first impressions of attractiveness are pretty accurate.
k Most participants ended up liking the same people in person as they did in the photos.

1 Two questions the studies investigated	a
2 Two reasons why the questions are important	
3 A description of how the studies are similar or different	
4 Five important points of the studies	
5 A comparison of the results of the two studies	

SPEAKING TASK

12 Imagine you are going to give a presentation about two research studies on navigation and cognitive health.

1 Read the information about the two studies.

2 Prepare talking points to explain the studies.

	Study 1	Study 2
research questions	Does the constant creation of mental maps affect cognition?	Can using GPS devices affect cognition?
important points	• A study compared London taxi drivers with a group of participants who did not drive taxis. • The hippocampi became much larger in the taxi drivers, and they did better on cognitive tests.	• One group navigated with spatial landmark strategy. The second group used GPS. • The first group had more grey matter and more activity in their hippocampi and performed better on cognitive tests.
points of similarity and contrast	• Both measured changes in the hippocampus; looked at the effects of using spatial memory on cognitive tests • Study 1: didn't consider effects of GPS	
results	• Study 1: shows likely causal relationship between the creation of mental maps and the increased size of the hippocampus • Study 2: doesn't show that GPS use is a definitive cause of lower test performance or that creating mental maps delays effects of ageing on cognition	

3 If you can work with another student or your teacher, give your presentation.
  • Follow the formal format for presentation of a research study.
  • Synthesize the important points of the two studies.
  • Discuss points of similarity and contrast.
  • Add emphasis to the focus words in thought groups.

UNIT 6 CAREERS

LISTENING

LISTENING FOR MAIN IDEAS

1 🔊 6.1 Listen to the conversation and tick ✔ the correct box for each sentence.

	true	false
1 Eva got a new job as a computer programmer.		
2 Eva had no help in preparing for her interview.		
3 Eva researched the company before her interview.		
4 Interviewers really want you to talk about how the job can help you achieve your goals.		
5 Soft skills are technical skills that help you do your job.		

LISTENING FOR DETAIL

2 🔊 6.1 Listen again and circle the correct phrases to complete the sentences.

1 Eva recently started working for *her dad / a small tech company / a big marketing company*.

2 Josh is preparing for *a job interview / his first day on the job / a meeting with a careers adviser*.

3 When asked 'Tell me about yourself,' Eva gave a summary of her *hobbies and interests / family background / accomplishments*.

4 The careers adviser suggested talking about how your skills and experience *are better than your classmates' / fit the needs of the company / will help you in your job*.

5 To research the company, Eva looked online and *visited their main office / called the human resources department / talked to someone who works there*.

6 Eva said that her biggest strength is being *analytical / collaborative / adaptable*.

7 Eva gave an example of a time she *handled an unexpected problem / completed an individual project / helped someone get a job*.

8 The question 'Why do you want this job?' gave Eva the chance to talk about *which computer programs she knew / what she knew and liked about the company / what her long-term career plans were*.

CAREERS UNIT 6

MAKING INFERENCES

3 🔊 **6.2** Listen and tick ✔ the correct sentence (a–c), using logic and your own knowledge to infer the speaker's meaning.

1
a ☐ You would expect this to be an easy question.
b ☐ This question is not easy enough to answer.
c ☐ Do you think this is an easy question?

2
a ☐ It was by chance that I met with a careers adviser.
b ☐ It was a good thing I was prepared for this question.
c ☐ It was lucky that I didn't ramble on.

3
a ☐ I can't believe you did all that work.
b ☐ I'm surprised your careers adviser gave you so much homework.
c ☐ I'm impressed you prepared so well.

4
a ☐ I guessed they wanted employees who can handle change well.
b ☐ I knew that the company would want me to work on a lot of projects.
c ☐ I realized they would want employees to change jobs.

5
a ☐ I think analytical and technical skills are more important than soft skills.
b ☐ I expected the company to be more concerned with analytical and technical skills.
c ☐ I don't think the company cares enough about analytical and technical skills.

LANGUAGE DEVELOPMENT

ACADEMIC VOCABULARY

4 Match the words (1–8) with their definitions (a–h).

1 distinct
2 dreaded
3 daunting
4 discrimination
5 analytical
6 reiterate
7 accomplishment
8 collaboration

a careful and systematic
b making you feel less confident; frightening
c cooperative effort
d unwelcome because of being unpleasant
e clearly separate and different
f something done successfully
g to repeat, usually using different words or phrasing
h unfair treatment, especially based on gender, ethnic origin, age or religion

5 Complete the sentences using the words and phrases in the box.

> wardrobe   format   get stuck with   ramble
> vision   hurry   rewarding   rehearsed

1 Research potential employers and positions carefully, or you may _____ a job you don't like.
2 Your career will be more _____ if you are able to use your strengths.
3 I need to update my _____ before I start my new job. All I have are old jeans and T-shirts.
4 You're going to have to _____ to get your research paper done on time. I told you to start it sooner, but you wouldn't listen.
5 The CEO has a _____ of where our company should be in five years' time.
6 I need to change the _____ of my CV. It isn't very easy to read.
7 I tend to _____ and talk too much when I'm nervous.
8 His responses to questions seemed awkward and _____ .

DEGREE EXPRESSIONS WITH *SO ... THAT*;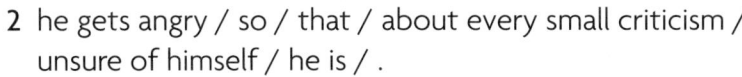
SUCH A ... THAT

6 Put the words in the correct order to make sentences.

1 applied / it took days / that / all the CVs / so many / for the position / people / to read / .
_____
_____

2 he gets angry / so / that / about every small criticism / unsure of himself / he is / .
_____
_____

3 a problem / he was fired / his behaviour / such / that / from / became / his last job / .
_____
_____

4 so / the streets / it rained / it flooded / hard / that / .
_____
_____

5 part time / a burden / was / she could only work / was / balancing work and motherhood / such / that / .
_____
_____

6 hired / that / the interviewer / such / she showed / skill and confidence / her / right then and there / .
_____
_____

7 Rewrite each pair of sentences (1–6) as a sentence, using the degree expression *so ... that* or *such (a) ... that*. For some sentences, more than one answer is possible.

1 The company made a big profit last year. It was able to employ thousands of new workers.
   The company made such a big profit last year that it was able to employ thousands of new workers.

2 I didn't go out at all last weekend. I had a lot of homework.

3 We forgot to lock the front door when we left. We were excited about going on holiday.

4 He accepted the position. The start-up offered him a large salary.

5 The thought of working for himself was daunting. He decided to take a corporate job.

6 He rambled on for a long time. He forgot the question he wanted to ask.

EMPHATIC EXPRESSIONS

8 Complete the sentences using the words and phrases in the box.

> without   by   to be   believe   make   without saying

1 _____ no mistake, you should consider your career choice very carefully.
2 Networking is a critical part of any job search, _____ me.
3 _____ a doubt, being flexible and willing to learn are valuable skills for any position.
4 It goes _____ that employers want workers they can trust.
5 _____ sure, you will be expected to collaborate with others in your new job.
6 _____ all means, send a thank-you note after the interview.

PRONUNCIATION

REDUCTION OF AUXILIARY VERBS

9 🔊 6.3 Listen to the sentences and write the full form of the reductions you hear.

1 I ____want to____ know what to expect.
2 You _____ be careful not to ramble on and on, without talking about what they really want to know.
3 The careers advisor _____ suggested researching the company and the position before the interview.
4 I _____ talk about how my skills and experience fit their needs.
5 What they really _____ know is what you can do for them.
6 I _____ tell she liked my answer.
7 I _____ thought they'd care more about being analytical.
8 Those kinds of skills are always _____ help you, no matter what job you do.
9 She also asked, 'Why _____ you want this job?'

SPEAKING

BODY LANGUAGE

10 Tick ✔ the correct box for each picture.

	positive body language	negative body language
1		
2		
3		
4		

CAREERS UNIT 6

11 Match the body language problems (1–4) with the pictures (a–d).

_____ 1 not standing up straight
_____ 2 not smiling
_____ 3 crossing your arms
_____ 4 not making eye contact

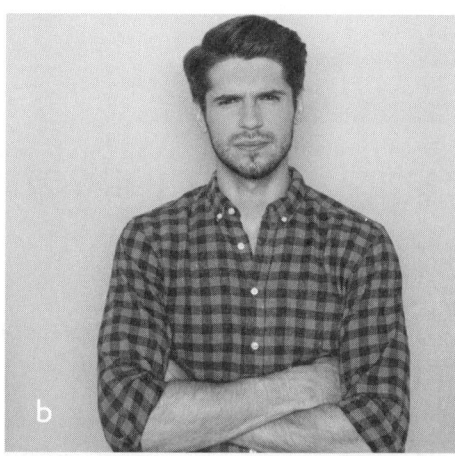

SPEAKING TASK

12 Imagine you have an interview for your dream job, and you need to prepare.

1 Prepare talking points to answer the following questions.
   - Tell me about yourself.
   - What is your biggest strength?
   - What is your biggest weakness?
   - Why do you want this job?
   - What questions do you have for me?

2 If you can work with another student or your teacher, practise the interview.
   - Make a good impression with your initial greeting.
   - Answer questions appropriately but concisely – don't ramble.
   - End the interview on a positive note.

UNIT 7 HEALTH

LISTENING

LISTENING TO INTRODUCTIONS

1 🔊 7.1 Listen to the introduction to a talk at a university. Circle the correct words and phrases to complete the sentences.

1 The speaker is a *doctor / professor / student*.
2 The topic of the talk is *hearing loss / throat problems / the elderly*.
3 Most people with hearing loss are *over sixty-five / under sixty-five / teens*.
4 The incidence of hearing loss in teens has increased by *ten / twenty / thirty* percent since the 1990s.
5 Nearly one in *three / five / nine* teens has some hearing loss.

LISTENING FOR DETAIL

2 🔊 7.2 Listen to the full presentation and circle the correct words to complete the sentences.

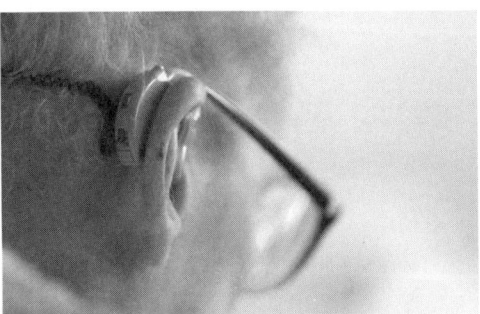 

1 Conductive hearing loss occurs when sound can't travel efficiently through the *ear drum / outer ear / inner ear*.
2 Sensorineural hearing loss occurs when there is damage to the *inner ear / middle ear / ear drum*.
3 Sensorineural hearing loss usually results in *temporary / permanent / correctable* loss of hearing.
4 Sensorineural hearing loss can often be prevented by *using a hearing aid / not listening to music / reducing exposure to noise*.
5 Noise levels at or below *60 / 75 / 85* decibels are considered safe for adults.
6 To protect your hearing, Dr Kumar recommends avoiding *headphones / earbuds / MP3 players*.

HEALTH UNIT 7

USING A GRAPHIC ORGANIZER TO CAPTURE DETAILS

3 🔊 **7.2** Listen again and complete the notes using the words and numbers in the box.

> hearing aids   corrected   8   headphones   fluid   60
> exposure   unclear   unit   loud noise   earbuds   85

main ideas	details
rate of hearing loss ↑ young people	• incidence ↑ 30% in teens since 90s • 1 in 5 teens some loss
conductive hearing loss	• sound can't travel through mid. ear • e.g. (1)_____ from ear infection, allergies • result: hear ↓ intensity/volume • can usually be (2)_____ w/surgery, meds.
sensorineural hearing Loss	• damage to inner ear, nerve pathways • causes: e.g. genetics, ageing, (3)_____ • result: sounds (4)_____ • ↑ young ppl • us. permanent • treatment: (5)_____
prevention	• reduce (6)_____ to noise • loss is graudual → realize too late

safe noise level	• decibel = (7)_____ of sound
	   • conversation = (8)_____ dB
	   • heavy traffic = (9)_____ dB
	   • MP3 player @ max = 100 dB
	• ≤ 75 dB = safe
	• limit: 85 dB/(10)_____ hrs; 100 dB/15 mins
	• ↑ sound, ↓ time for damage

audio devices	• 60/60 rule: volume ≤ 60% of maximum ≤ 60 mins/day • over-ear (11)_____ better • (12)_____ – sound too close to eardrum; bad at filtering noise → unsafe • concert – use ear plugs

LANGUAGE DEVELOPMENT

UNIT VOCABULARY

4 Complete the crossword puzzle.

Across
2 Qualities that make something useful in a particular way (10)
4 In a way that is opposite of what is expected (10)
6 An established procedure (8)
7 Related to the national government (7)
8 The rate at which something happens (9)

Down
1 Unequally (18)
3 Cleanliness (7)
5 Nearness (9)

5 Complete the sentences using the words in the box.

> compromised   disparity   minimal   intervened
> correlation   contaminated   deprived   concentration

1 There is a _____ between income and life expectancy. Those with higher incomes are likely to live longer than those with lower incomes.
2 The _____ between the life expectancies of rich and poor is growing. Today, men in the top ten percent of income level live an average of 14 years longer than men in the bottom ten percent.
3 Many governments have made _____ effort to solve this problem. They could do much more.
4 Without health insurance, people in some countries are _____ of access to routine healthcare. They can't afford to visit a doctor.
5 In 2014, the drinking water in Flint, Michigan, was _____ with lead. As a result, thousands of children have suffered from lead poisoning.
6 The _____ of lead in the water was found to be at unsafe levels. The water in some households qualified to be labelled 'toxic waste'.
7 The quality of the water was so _____ that the city was declared to be in a federal state of emergency.
8 In 2016, a team of 300 plumbers _____ to install free water filters in the homes of Flint residents.

ESTABLISHING COHESION WITH *SO*

6 Put the words in the correct order to make sentences.

1 exposure to / and / genetics can cause / so / hearing loss, / can / loud noise / . _____

2 doing / reduced / so, / of hearing loss / playing his music too loudly, / he stopped / and / by / his risk / . _____

3 countless other musicians / noise-induced hearing loss, / have / has suffered from / and / so / guitarist Pete Townshend / . _____

4 ear plugs / and / at the concert, / did / I decided / so / my friend / to wear / . _____

5 their hearing, / young children / and / teens are losing / so / are / . _____

ESTABLISHING COHESION WITH *SUCH*

7 Read the information. Rewrite the second sentence using *such*.

1. Some companies are manufacturing headphones that restrict volume levels. Headphones like the ones just mentioned may help prevent hearing loss in children.
   Such headphones may help prevent hearing loss in children.

2. One study found that half of children's headphones tested did not restrict volume as promised. Studies like the one just mentioned should be a warning to parents to research headphones before buying them.
   _____
   _____

3. One set of headphones reached 114 decibels. A volume level like the one just mentioned can damage hearing within minutes.
   _____
   _____

4. Some headphones advertise themselves as 'one hundred percent safe'. There is no headphone in existence like the ones just mentioned.
   _____
   _____

5. Some children listen for hours at a time. Intense listening like that can also cause damage.
   _____
   _____

ADJECTIVES OF STRONG DISAPPROVAL

8 Circle the correct adjectives to complete the sentences.

1. The lead levels in the water were *appalling / appalled*.
2. Scientists were *dismayed / atrocious* when they saw the test results.
3. The public was *outraged / outrageous* by the lack of attention to the problem.
4. In 1986, the world learned the *horrifying / horrified* news of the Chernobyl nuclear disaster.
5. Even more *shocking / outraged* was the fact that the public was not immediately notified, placing many people in danger of radiation poisoning.
6. My mother was *horrified / dreadful* when she saw my room at university.
7. She couldn't believe the *deplorable / aghast* conditions.

PRONUNCIATION

CONTRASTIVE STRESS

9 🔊 **7.3** Listen and underline things which are contrasted in each item 1–4. Underline no more than four words in each sentence.

1 We all know the stereotype of the <u>elderly</u> person who is hard of hearing, but ironically, the majority of people with hearing loss are <u>younger than sixty-five</u>.
2 Today, the rate of hearing loss in teens is thirty percent higher than it was in the 1990s.
3 Unlike conductive hearing loss, sensorineural hearing loss can result in sounds being unclear, even when they are loud enough.
4 A normal conversation is about sixty decibels, while noise from heavy city traffic is about eight-five decibels.

SPEAKING

INCLUSIVE LANGUAGE

10 Complete the inclusive statements using words and phrases from the box. You do not need to use all the words and phrases.

> us   ours   our   don't you   aren't you   everyone   me   we

1 I am deeply concerned about the safety of this power plant. _____ ?
2 Like _____ , I want to know that our community is safe.
3 _____ all deserve answers to these questions.
4 Every one of _____ should stand up and demand action.
5 _____ children are counting on us to protect them.
6 I feel it is our duty to protect the environment for future generations. _____ ?

PERSUASIVE APPEALS

11 For each sentence (1–8), tick ✔ the box that describes the type of persuasive appeal being used.

	appeal for trust	appeal to emotion	appeal to logic
1 I have been a city water inspector for more than 20 years.			
2 Scientists have found dangerously high levels of lead in our water, which must be dealt with immediately.			
3 It's clear we must act immediately in order to prevent further damage to the water system and to minimize health risks.			
4 Children's lives are at stake here. We need to act now.			
5 As a resident and community leader, I care deeply about the health and safety of everyone who lives here.			
6 This situation is simply appalling. We must do all that we can to remedy it.			
7 There is no safe blood lead level for children. Thus, we cannot allow any lead in our drinking water.			
8 In my role as a federal health official, I have helped many other communities deal with similar crises.			

SPEAKING TASK

12 Imagine you are participating in a community meeting to discuss a local environmental health crisis. You are going to present the position of someone involved with and/or affected by the problem.

1 Choose a community health problem.
- Contaminated water
- Air or noise pollution
- Other: _____

2 Prepare talking points to explain your position.
- Prepare a position statement.
- Acknowledge the motivation and objections of others.
- Use inclusive language to gain support for your position.

3 If you can work with another student or your teacher, give your presentation.
- Use adjectives of strong emotion where appropriate.
- Appeal for trust, to emotion, or to logic, as appropriate.

UNIT 8 COLLABORATION

LISTENING

LISTENING FOR MAIN IDEAS

1 🔊 8.1 Listen to a student presentation on collaboration. Tick ✔ the correct box for each sentence.

	true	false
1 According to the speaker, collaboration is increasing in schools and workplaces.		
2 The speaker believes that working collaboratively is faster than working alone.		
3 Studies show that people don't try as hard when they work in groups.		
4 Researchers found that collaboration helps groups find better solutions.		
5 Researchers have found that collaborative groups tend to share work evenly.		

LISTENING FOR DETAIL

2 🔊 8.1 Listen to the presentation again and circle the correct words to complete the sentences.

1 Psychologists found that people *work faster / remember better / make better decisions* when they believe they are working alone to complete a task.
2 'Social loafing' means people don't work as hard when they think others *have a stake / waste time / are distracted* in completing their work.
3 When a 'group mind' develops, outcomes depend more on group *dynamics / intelligence / skill level* than anything else.
4 One study found that up to one-third of successful collaborations came from *twenty-five / three to five / thirty-five* percent of employees.
5 The speaker feels that collaboration is often unfair to people who are *shy / energetic / social*.
6 According to the speaker, collaboration can be helpful for certain tasks, such as *problem-solving / brainstorming / decision-making*.

UNDERSTANDING PROVERBS

3 🔊 **8.2** Listen to the proverb or expression in context. Tick ✔ the best explanation for it (a–c).

1 Too many cooks spoil the broth.
   a ☐ Having too many people involved in a task can result in the task taking too long to complete.
   b ☐ Too many opinions, even if they're good, can combine to make a bad result.
   c ☐ People should always work alone to complete a task.

2 Two heads are better than one.
   a ☐ Working with another person is more effective for problem solving than working alone.
   b ☐ It's better to have two possible solutions to one problem than just one solution.
   c ☐ People should always try to get along to solve problems.

3 Pull your own weight.
   a ☐ Do your work separately.
   b ☐ Refuse to work with others.
   c ☐ Do your fair share of the work.

4 Pick up the slack.
   a ☐ Do the work that someone else has stopped doing.
   b ☐ Teach someone how to do their work.
   c ☐ Choose the tasks that need to be done.

5 Burn out.
   a ☐ Get angry about problems that arise.
   b ☐ Become exhausted due to overwork.
   c ☐ Spend too much time working.

6 Throw the baby out with the bath water.
   a ☐ Get rid of something good along with something bad.
   b ☐ Clear your mind of all distractions.
   c ☐ Ignore anything that interferes with your work.

LANGUAGE DEVELOPMENT

UNIT VOCABULARY

4 Match the words and phrases (1–8) with their definitions (a–h).

1 counteract
2 defuse
3 prevail
4 resentment
5 stake
6 tinker
7 hybrid
8 sense of ownership

a to become dominant; to win in the end
b a make small changes in order to improve something
c a feeling of responsibility for something connected to you but not yours
d a personal interest or investment
e something that is a combination of two or more things
f to make a situation calmer or less dangerous
g to reduce the negative effect of something
h anger at being forced to accept something you don't like

5 Complete the sentences using the words in the box.

> resolve   insight   constructive   perception
> outcome   consensus   dynamics   reservations

1 My teacher is good at giving _____ feedback that helps me understand how to improve.
2 We should improve the _____ within our team. We need to communicate better if we want to achieve our goals.
3 The research study provided valuable _____ into the ways men and women sometimes communicate differently. We've redesigned our survey questions to account for that.
4 Many people have the _____ that two heads are better than one, but that isn't always true.
5 I am happy with the _____ of our meeting. I think we came up with good solutions to our problems.
6 I have some _____ about this plan, but I'm willing to give it a try and see what happens.
7 It took several hours of discussion, but we finally reached a _____ .
8 There is one issue that we were unable to _____ . We will have to continue our discussion in order to find a solution.

WH- CLEFTS

6 Put the words in the correct order to make sentences with *what* clefts.

1 collaboration / was / the study / can lead to / what / 'social loafing' / showed / that / .

2 saying / people / as hard / in groups / what / you're / is / don't work / ?

3 that / don't want / what / me / surprises / to help others more / is / people / .

4 don't understand / reached / how / what / those conclusions / I / is / you / .

5 the most capable / burn-out / employees / saying / that / what / is / suffer / they're / .

6 that / become exhausted / mean / what / the best workers / you / is / ?

7 found / employee engagement / what / a decrease in / the researchers / was / .

7 Rewrite the sentences (1–6) as questions or statements, using *wh*-cleft sentences to clarify them. Use the words in brackets in the clefts. More than one answer may be possible.

1 I think we should consider some other options. (I / say)
   <u>What I'm saying is I think we should consider some other options.</u>

2 These results are wrong? (you / say?)

3 We should look at them more carefully. (I / mean)

4 People come up with better ideas when they work alone. (you / mean?)

5 You are too shy to give your opinions in a group. (you / tell me?)

6 No one in the team likes to work with him. (I / tell you)

COLLOCATIONS: PREPOSITIONS

8 Match the sentence halves.

_____ 1 Let's concentrate
_____ 2 You can count
_____ 3 You can plan
_____ 4 The client didn't like our proposal. We need to come up
_____ 5 I think it's useless to engage
_____ 6 That solution will result
_____ 7 I don't know how to deal
_____ 8 We need to develop a business plan that is consistent

a in more problems. We need to think of something else.
b on delays. There's a lot of construction on the highway near there.
c with another idea. Any suggestions?
d with our mission.
e on me to finish my share of the work.
f in discussion about ideas we're not going to pursue. Let's use our time for real possibilities.
g with him. He always dominates the discussion.
h on getting our work done.

PRONUNCIATION

CONTRACTED FORMS OF *WILL*

9 🔊 8.3 Listen and circle the words that you hear.

1 *It'll / It will* take longer to reach consensus than *it'll / it will* to decide individually.
2 I know *what'll / what will* happen if we work together. *I'll / I will* end up doing most of the work.
3 Maybe the others won't help, but *I'll / I will*. *We'll / We will* finish it together.
4 **A:** Will you please give me a hand with this?
  B: I can't, but I'm sure *Paul'll / Paul will* once he gets home.
5 Our *group'll / group will* report our results tomorrow. *When'll / When will* your group be ready?

SPEAKING

COLLABORATIVE LANGUAGE: SUGGESTION AND CONCESSION

10 Complete the sentences using words and phrases from the box. You do not need to use all the words and phrases. More than one answer may be possible.

> propose that   consider   why   what
> willing   how   suggest   understand

1 _____ about placing the facility outside town?
2 _____ don't we try placing extra police in the area?
3 What do you _____ ?
4 I _____ we develop job training programmes for the former prisoners.
5 _____ about giving them volunteer jobs in the community?
6 I _____ this isn't the best solution, but it's the best we can come up with.

11 Rewrite the sentences using the phrase in brackets and changing the underlined part of each sentence to a suggestion or a concession.

1 <u>This policy is harsh</u>, but it's the best way to prevent plagiarism. (I admit)
   <u>I admit that this policy is harsh, but it's the best way to prevent plagiarism.</u>

2 <u>I want to place</u> the students on probation. (How about / ?)
   _____
   _____

3 <u>We need to set up</u> a system to track repeat offences of plagiarism. (Let's try) _____

4 <u>I will only</u> support this proposal if we require tutors to report plagiarism. (I would be willing)
   _____
   _____

5 <u>I want to provide</u> workshops to all students on how to avoid plagiarism. (Why don't we consider / ?)
   _____
   _____

6 <u>This proposal</u> is not perfect, but <u>I want you</u> to support it. (I understand that / would you be willing / anyway?)
   _____
   _____

SPEAKING TASK

12 Imagine you are preparing to participate in a consensus-building decision-making task. You need to choose one of three options for solving a budget crisis at your university and present your proposed solution.

1 Read the scenario and the three proposed solutions.

Scenario
Your university has announced that, due to budget cuts, it needs to raise money to cover expenses for the following year. Currently, there are three proposed solutions.

Proposal 1	Proposal 2	Proposal 3
This proposal would raise student tuition fees by 3%. Some of the money would go towards financial aid for students unable to pay for the increased tuition cost.	This proposal would eliminate pay rises for full-time staff who earn £45,000 a year or more. The extra funds would go towards offering more courses taught by part-time staff, who earn an average of £15,000.	This proposal would eliminate pay rises for university administrators, including the vice-chancellor, who earns £150,000 a year, and deans, who earn an average of £70,000 a year. Some of the money would be used to hire more full-time staff.

2 Choose a proposal and prepare talking points to explain your position.

3 If you can work with another student or your teacher, give your presentation.
- Prepare a position statement.
- Offer a cost–benefit analysis of the proposal that you support.
- Anticipate how you will respond to competing proposals.
- Use collaborative language for making suggestions and offering concessions in your anticipated responses.

UNIT 9 TECHNOLOGY

LISTENING

PREDICTING CONTENT FROM VISUALS

1 Look at the photographs and circle the statement you believe to be correct.

    a You can play music on all of these items.
    b All of these items can send and receive information via the internet.
    c You can only find these items in a large city.
    d All of these items are household appliances.

LISTENING FOR MAIN IDEAS

2 🔊 9.1 Listen to the radio programme and put the main ideas in the order (1–6) that they are mentioned.

    _____ The risks associated with internet-connected devices
    _____ A definition of the Internet of Things
    _____ Examples of internet-connected devices
    _____ The digital divide that internet-connected devices could lead to
    _____ The convenience that internet-connected devices offer
    _____ The safety aspect of internet-connected devices

LISTENING FOR DETAIL

3 🔊 9.1 Listen again and complete the notes.

- No. of internet-connected devices: approx. 50 (1)_____
- Internet of Things: everyday objects which can send and receive (2)_____ via the internet
- Examples:
  - (3)_____ – tell the time and read emails or surf the internet
  - fitness trackers – measure steps walked, (4)_____ burned and exercise completed
  - modern household devices, e.g. lights, heating, (5)_____ and washing machines
  - doorbells / CCTV cameras that let you see who's at your door
  - car trackers – diagnose problems with the car and inform (6)_____ of an accident
- Positives:
  - safety
  - security of your (7)_____
- Negatives:
  - security – risk to your privacy
  - digital (8)_____ between those who know how everything works and those who don't

LANGUAGE DEVELOPMENT

ACADEMIC VOCABULARY

4 Rewrite the sentences, replacing the words in brackets with the correct word or phrase from the box.

> remotely   monitor   GPS   digital divide
> have the security of knowing   drawbacks

1 A smartwatch can also function as a (device which shows your position by using signals from satellites).

2 You can control your washing machine (from a distance via your smartphone).

3 If your car's performance is being tracked, you (can relax as you can be sure) that you will be alerted before something goes wrong.

4 As with all new developments, internet connectivity also has some (disadvantages).

5 The more opportunities companies have to (watch) your activities for a period of time, the more they will know about you.

6 As we get more computer technology and internet-connected devices, the (difference between people who understand how internet technology works and those who don't) is likely to become even greater.

5 Read the clues and find the words in the word search.

1 Having a human form: h_____ (8)
2 A fear of technology: t_____ (12)
3 The first example of something, such as a machine or other industrial product, from which all later forms are developed: p_____ (9)
4 People who resent new technology and are usually the last to adopt it: l_____ (8)
5 The first people to adopt new technology: i_____ (10)
6 The ability to perform a difficult action quickly and skilfully with the hands, or the ability to think quickly and effectively: d_____ (9)
7 A strong feeling of sympathy and sadness for the suffering or bad luck of others and a wish to help them: c_____ (10)

W	E	A	D	O	L	N	Y	R	Y	O	Z	G	V	I
G	U	N	E	A	I	F	V	Y	S	N	X	F	G	N
J	F	A	X	S	K	R	H	Y	D	X	M	P	M	N
W	J	F	T	A	U	D	C	Y	F	Q	T	R	J	O
P	X	K	E	I	W	N	O	X	Z	T	H	O	Z	V
O	Z	K	R	K	R	L	M	X	P	O	K	T	F	A
A	W	L	I	G	N	W	P	S	Q	R	X	O	X	T
L	Q	W	T	W	J	M	A	D	T	P	Z	T	K	O
A	K	A	Y	Z	M	F	S	Z	F	Q	X	Y	A	R
G	P	V	Q	J	X	O	S	K	W	I	G	P	Q	S
G	H	U	M	A	N	O	I	D	D	X	L	E	U	D
A	C	T	E	C	H	N	O	P	H	O	B	I	A	L
R	F	D	N	Q	K	Y	N	S	A	P	J	G	C	L
D	R	E	T	B	K	Z	O	X	G	D	G	O	M	G
S	M	N	O	V	H	L	T	H	X	X	J	F	K	H

NEGATIVE PREFIXES

6 Circle the correct words to complete the sentences.

1 Whenever I have to talk to machines, for instance, on the phone, I find it very *impersonal / immobile*.
2 Once AI starts to become part of our everyday lives, the process will almost certainly be *irreversible / irrational*.
3 The Internet of Things will soon be *undesirable / unavoidable* – we will all end up controlling something via the internet.
4 Humans can be very *unsustainable / unproductive* if they are not completely focussed on their work, but this doesn't happen with robots.
5 Being afraid of any new technology without considering its benefits and drawbacks is *irrational / irrevocable*.
6 The more internet-connected devices we have in the future, the greater the risk that *unscrupulous / unproductive* individuals may monitor our activity.
7 Just 50 years ago, all of today's technological developments probably seemed completely *imperfect / implausible*, but today they are reality.
8 As soon as a new technological development has been adopted by an early majority, its large-scale adoption is *irrevocable / irreplaceable*.

7 Complete the sentences using the words in the box.

> imperfect   immoral   irrespective
> unsustainable   undesirable   irreplaceable

1 Some people thought that the idea of the internet was _____ and now we are looking at having even the most everyday objects linked to it.
2 It is argued that there will always be jobs where humans are _____ .
3 _____ of the fact that technology is all around us, there are still a lot of people who are not familiar with it.
4 Despite the fact that we are making huge progress in robotics, many people argue that robots will always be _____ compared to humans.
5 Scientists believe that it is _____ to create humanoid robots which are as tall as humans because this will make us feel uncomfortable.
6 There are concerns that drones and humanoid robots may be used for _____ or illegal purposes.

TECHNOLOGY   UNIT 9

HYPOTHETICAL FUTURE

8 Write hypothetical future sentences, using the correct form of the verbs in brackets. You will need to put some verbs into the passive voice.

1 Many people (be) afraid that their personal information might be accessible if all their everyday devices (link) to the internet.
   <u>Many people would be afraid that their personal information might be accessible if all their everyday devices were linked to the internet.</u>

2 I (hate) to be in a situation where robots (become) our everyday servants.

3 It (be) difficult to imagine a world in which all cars (control) by computers.

4 If all cars (drive) by computers, there (probably be) fewer accidents.

5 I wonder how people (make) a living if most jobs (do) by robots.

6 It (be) strange to consider a world in which you (walk) into a supermarket and the only customers (be) humanoid robots doing the shopping for their humans.

PRONUNCIATION

ELISION

9 🔊 **9.2** Listen and mark on the paragraph seven examples of elision within words or across word boundaries. The first one has been done for you as an example.

> I hope you all had a chance to read‿the articles for today's seminar. With the recent advances in robotics, the issue of AI taking over human jobs has caused a great deal of concern. We all know that robots work in factory assembly lines, manufacturing cars and computer chips. In some places, robots are used as prison guards. Restaurants in different parts of the world employ robots to take orders and serve food. Humanoid robots have been used to man reception desks and interact with customers.

SPEAKING

INTERACTIONAL DISCOURSE MARKERS

10 Complete the conversation using the discourse markers in the box. You can use some words and phrases more than once. More than one answer may be possible.

> you know   really   I see   say   yeah   right   actually   well

Tutor: (1)_____ , ok, so today we are going to be talking about developments in technology. What is the latest technological item you bought? Adam?

Adam: (2)_____ , I bought a new smartphone last week.

Tutor: (3)_____ ? OK, and how is it different to your previous phone?

Adam: (4)_____ , it is not very different – it is just a newer model with a better camera.

Tutor: (5)_____ . Good, thanks. Has anyone else bought any new technology recently?

Sarah: (6)_____ , I have.

Tutor: (7)_____ . What did you buy, Sarah?

Sarah: I bought a new 2-in-1 laptop, (8)_____ one of those where you can use it as a tablet or a laptop.

Tutor: Wow! Lucky you! They're great. OK, I want you to work in pairs now and discuss what you would buy if you had, (9)_____ , 3,000 dollars to spend on new technology – of any type. Have a quick think about it and then discuss with your partner what you would buy and why …

ASKING FOR CLARIFICATION AND CONFIRMATION

11 🔊 9.3 Listen to the extracts from conversations about technology and decide whether the second speaker requests clarification, or paraphrases and asks for confirmation. Tick ✔ the correct box for each extract.

	clarification	paraphrase and confirmation
1		✔
2		
3		
4		
5		
6		

SPEAKING TASK

12 Imagine you are going to take part in an informal discussion on the following topic:

The Internet of Things: a positive contribution to our lives or a huge risk to our privacy and security?

1 Choose one of the positions.

   Position A
   You support the idea that the Internet of Things is a positive contribution to our lives.

   Position B
   You support the argument that the Internet of Things is a huge risk to our privacy and security.

2 Prepare for the discussion.
   - Present and justify arguments for your position.
   - Think of one idea that could be presented for the other position, and how you could paraphrase it and ask for confirmation.
   - Think of how you might ask for clarification at least once during the discussion.

3 If you can work with another student or your teacher, have the discussion.
   - Remember to paraphrase and ask for confirmation.
   - Remember to ask for clarification.

UNIT 10 LANGUAGE

LISTENING

LISTENING FOR MAIN IDEAS

1. 🔊 10.1 Listen to a group discussion. Tick ✔ the topics they discuss.
   a ☐ Food and drink
   b ☐ Transport and travel
   c ☐ Family members
   d ☐ History
   e ☐ Colours
   f ☐ Politics

ACTIVATING YOUR KNOWLEDGE

2. 🔊 10.1 Listen to the classroom discussion. Tick ✔ the correct box for each word.

	Spanish	Russian	Arabic
mummy			
cargo			
cosmonaut			
embargo			
armadillo			
gazelle			
beluga			
mammoth			

LANGUAGE UNIT 10

LISTENING FOR DETAIL

3 🔊 10.1 Listen again and complete the student's notes with the information that you hear.

History
- Arabic words
  - Alhambra
    - meaning: The Red One
    - also used in: Spanish
  - sultan
    - meaning: ruler
  - mummy
    - meaning: a dead body which has been (1) _____
  - also used in: Russian, German

Transport and travel
- Arabic words
  - tare (weight)
    - meaning: weight of something when empty
- Spanish words
  - (2) _____
    - root: from 'cargar' = to carry
    - meaning: freight
- Russian words
  - cosmonaut
    - root: Greek words (3) _____ and 'nautes'
  - sputnik
    - meaning: a Soviet space satellite

Politics
- Russian words:
  - perestroika
  - glasnost
  - Bolshevik
- Spanish words
  - embargo
    - meaning: to (4) _____

Food and drink
- Spanish words
  - paella
  - fajitas
  - tapas
  - cafeteria
    - also used in: (5) _____, but usually shortened to café.
- Arabic words
  - sugar
  - (6) _____

Animals
- Spanish words
  - armadillo
    - meaning: small mammal with hard plates on its back
    - root: 'armado' = armed and the diminutive '-illo' meaning 'little'
- Arabic words
  - (7) _____
  - gazelle
- Russian words
  - beluga
    - meaning: a type of whale
    - also used in: Spanish
- mammoth
  - meaning: large prehistoric mammal

Other
- Arabic words
  - check
    - root: 'Shah' = Persian for 'king'
  - checkmate
    - root: 'shah mat' – meaning: king dead
    - similar words used in: (8) _____ and (9) _____

LANGUAGE DEVELOPMENT

UNIT VOCABULARY

4 Complete the sentences using the words in the box.

> grasp   aptitude   complexities   literally
> coherent   frustrating   excel   intrinsic

1 The _____ of different language mean that it is difficult for a machine to produce a _____ translation.
2 Students who have a high level of _____ motivation are often successful language learners.
3 People with a particular _____ for a certain subject usually _____ in those subjects.
4 Armadillo _____ means a small animal whose body is covered in armour – hard plates which protect it.
5 It can be very _____ if you cannot _____ a particular grammar point.

5 Complete the crossword puzzle.

Across
2 My friend gave me e_____ instructions about how to find her house but we still managed to get lost. (8)
4 The student failed the exam because his answers were completely i_____ . (16)
5 Different linguists have r_____ different ideas about how people learn languages. (9)
7 There was a d_____ between the machine translation and the human translation. (11)
8 Some students are not r_____ interested in languages because they do not see the value in being able to speak another language. (8)

Down
1 In some situations, it can be difficult to d_____ the right course of action. (9)
3 The party was planned so s_____ that nothing could possibly go wrong. (14)
6 The students were able to u_____ the online dictionaries to help them with their essays. (7)

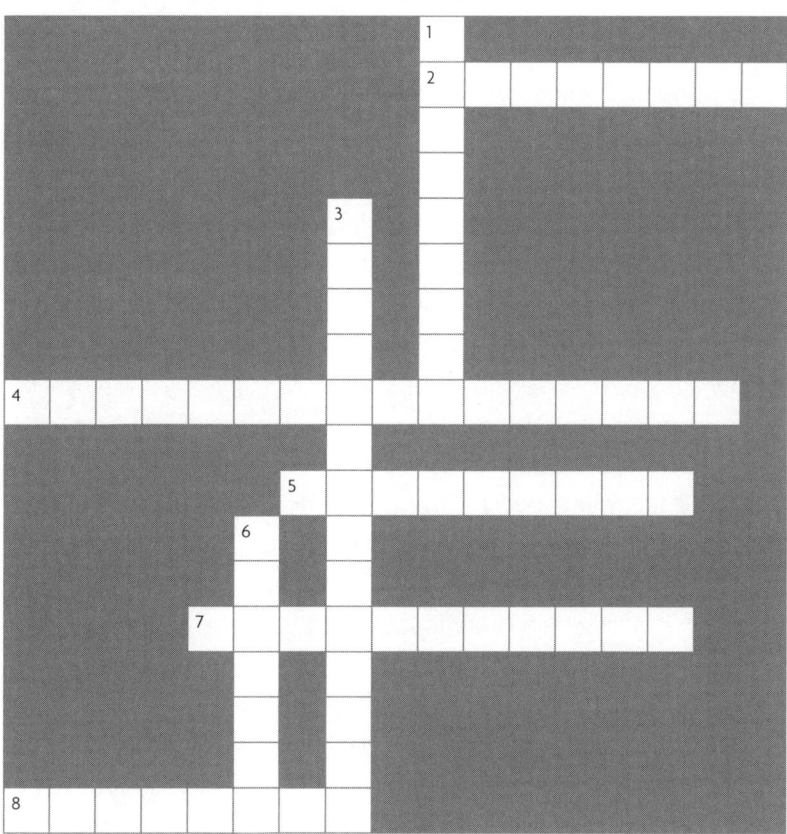

PHRASAL VERBS

6 Complete the sentences with the correct preposition(s) to complete the phrasal verbs.

1 Tim is a great speaker. He always comes __across__ as extremely knowledgeable.
2 This discussion is very interesting but we need to move _____, otherwise we will run out of time.
3 I have a few questions about my assignment. Could I talk it _____ with you, please?
4 John is going to Russia soon, so he will have to brush _____ the language before he goes.
5 When my parents think _____ how they learnt foreign languages, they say it was much more difficult to practise because they didn't have access to the different language learning apps that exist now.
6 I can't work _____ how to access the Learning Management System. Can you help me, please?
7 Social media accounts _____ a considerable proportion of exposure to foreign languages outside the classroom.

COMPLEX GERUND AND INFINITIVE PHRASES

7 Circle the correct words to complete the sentences.

I began learning German when I went to university as a mature student at the age of 30. ⁽¹⁾*Having struggled with French at school / To have struggled with French at school*, I decided to challenge myself ⁽²⁾*learning a foreign language / to learn a foreign language*. I had spent a few months ⁽³⁾*learning German at night school / to learn German at night school* before ⁽⁴⁾*starting university / to start university* so I hoped that this would give me a head start. As part of my degree course, I went to Austria for a year ⁽⁵⁾*developing my language skills / to develop my language skills* and then went back to finish my degree. ⁽⁶⁾*Having graduated with a degree in German / To have graduated with a degree in German*, I moved back to Austria and did a translation qualification. I have been working as a technical translator for over 20 years now! ⁽⁷⁾*Thinking back to my time in school / To think back to my time in school*, I don't know why I struggled so much with French – perhaps I was just lacking the motivation or perhaps I just had a very good German teacher! The point is that it is possible ⁽⁸⁾*achieving your goal / to achieve your goal* if you set your heart on it!

LANGUAGE — UNIT 10

8 Rewrite the sentences, replacing the words in brackets with a complex gerund or infinitive.

1 (I had studied Spanish in school so) I decided to continue to study it at university.
   <u>Having studied Spanish in school, I decided to continue to study it at university.</u>

2 (I had spent a few months in Seville) before (I moved to Cádiz so) I was already used to the Andulusian accent when I got there.

3 (When I look back to my primary school education), I realize we didn't study any foreign languages back then. What a wasted opportunity!

4 Louisa decided (that she would use an online translation machine) for her homework, but the result was so bad that she could have done better herself!

PRONUNCIATION

LINKING AND CATENATION

9 🔊 10.2 Listen and underline eight examples of consonant + vowel sound linking.

> I remember tha<u>t I</u> had Russian friends visiting once. I wanted to send them directions to my house. I used an internet translation app to translate my directions from English to Russian and then I sent them to my friends. I can't read Russian so I had no idea what it said.

10 🔊 **10.3** Listen and complete the sentences with the words you hear.

> That is ⁽¹⁾_____ . Vocabulary-related problems account for the biggest ⁽²⁾_____ the development of machine translation. In fact, ⁽³⁾_____ to determine which sense or meaning of a word to use has been ⁽⁴⁾_____ the biggest challenges faced by scientists ⁽⁵⁾_____ developing machine translation programmes since the 1950s. IBM was the first company to launch a machine translation programme, known as 'the brain'. In those days, IBM scientists claimed that to ⁽⁶⁾_____ a small section of text required more programming than it took to simulate the ⁽⁷⁾_____ guided missile.

SPEAKING

INTERRUPTING AND HANDLING QUESTIONS

11 🔊 **10.4** Listen to the conversation about the Critical Age Hypothesis. Complete the conversation with the phrases the speakers use to interrupt and handle questions.

Speaker 1: I was just reading about the Critical Age Hypothesis. Have you heard of it? It suggests that there is a certain age after which it is impossible to learn a language to a native-like proficiency. The research evidence is really fascinating. I am not sure whether I agree with it or not.

Speaker 2: ⁽¹⁾_____ we can only learn language to a high level if we are below a certain age?

Speaker 1: Well, that is what the theory suggests. ⁽²⁾_____ the research evidence is fascinating but there are arguments on both sides. Some researchers argue that the critical age can be as low as three, for example, to get a perfect accent, but others argue it may be around age thirteen. Opponents of the Critical Age Hypothesis suggest it is linked to other factors such as time available to learn and motivation.

Speaker 3: ⁽³⁾_____ I'm not clear on the age range. How can some people argue that the critical age is three while others say it is thirteen?

Speaker 1: Researchers look at different aspects of language learning – for example, pronunciation, where they say the age is younger, or grammatical features, where the age is higher. (4)_____ there are interesting studies for both sides of the argument …

Speaker 2: (5)_____ but I am not convinced that there is a critical age. I know a lot of adults who speak foreign languages very well – to the point that you wouldn't know they were non-native speakers.

Speaker 3: Yes, but they don't usually have a perfect accent – you can usually tell they are non-native speakers. On the other hand, people who have grown up in the country usually have a perfect native-speaker accent.

Speaker 1: (6)_____ – that there are plausible arguments on both sides …

SPEAKING TASK

12 Imagine you are going to interview a person on the following topic:

English has a lot of loanwords (words taken from other languages), and other languages also borrow from English. Do you think each language should create its own words, or is it better to borrow words from other languages?

1 Prepare for the interview.
   - Think about your own opinion on the topic.
   - Think of some reasons why your interviewee might have a different opinion.
   - Think about the language you will use if you need to interrupt during the conversation, and the language you will use if you are interrupted.

2 If you can work with another student or your teacher, do the interview. Interrupt the speaker at least twice during the interview.

UNITS 1–10 AUDIO SCRIPTS

UNIT 1

Host: Good afternoon and welcome to today's show. This week we're celebrating International Dark Sky Week. What is International Dark Sky Week? It was first established in 2003 by secondary school student Jennifer Barlow, and has since become an annual global event that takes place every April. Its goal? To help draw attention to the problem of light pollution and promote ways to combat it. So, what exactly is light pollution? Light pollution is the brightening of the night sky caused by man-made lights, such as street and building lights. Large cities obviously produce the most light pollution, but with increased development, this problem is accelerating and now affects eighty percent of the world's population. Here to tell us more is astronomer Melanie Turow. Welcome.

Host: Good afternoon and welcome to today's show. This week we're celebrating International Dark Sky Week. What is International Dark Sky Week? It was first established in 2003 by secondary school student Jennifer Barlow, and has since become an annual global event that takes place every April. It's goal? To help draw attention to the problem of light pollution and promote ways to combat it. So, what exactly is light pollution? Light pollution is the brightening of the night sky caused by man-made lights, such as street and building lights. Large cities obviously produce the most light pollution, but with increased development, this problem is accelerating and now affects eighty percent of the world's population. Here to tell us more is astronomer Melanie Turow. Welcome.

Melanie: Thanks for having me.

Host: Astronomers study stars and deep space. Why are you interested in light pollution here on Earth?

Melanie: Because of light pollution, astronomers are finding it increasingly difficult to see and study objects in the night sky. But light pollution actually affects all of us. Think about it. When was the last time you looked up and saw a sky full of stars? Well, fewer than a hundred years ago, everyone could look up and see a starry night sky. But now, many people around the world never have that experience.

Host: Yeah, you're right. Most of us who live in the city probably never think about it, but I can remember as a kid being able to look up and see lots of stars, even the Milky Way.

Melanie: Right, and now millions of children will never see the Milky Way. It's shameful, really. We're losing an important experience as human beings on this planet.

Host: So, are there other negative effects of light pollution?

Melanie: Yes, actually there are many ways that light pollution harms both humans and the environment. First of all, most lighting is just wasteful and uses too much energy.

Host: But aren't lights necessary for safety, especially in cities?

Melanie: I'm glad you brought that up. Actually, there's no evidence that increased lighting reduces crime in cities. In fact, too much lighting can cause problems, because lights that are too bright can shine in our eyes making it even more difficult to see. And artificial light can interfere with our natural ability to sleep at night. Loss of sleep is a big public health problem.

Host: Hmm ... good point. And what about environmental problems caused by light pollution?

Melanie: Unfortunately, wildlife and ecosystems also suffer from light pollution. Plants and animals depend on the daily cycle of light and darkness, and artificial light at night can have serious – even deadly – effects. For example, animals that rely on darkness to hide are now more vulnerable to predators and accidental death.

Host: Are there any particular species of animals that are threatened by light pollution?

Melanie: Yes, there are. Sea turtles. Nearly all species of sea turtles are endangered, and artificial lights are contributing to this problem.

Host: How's that?

Melanie: Baby sea turtles hatch from their eggs on beaches and usually leave their nests at night. They're naturally drawn to light – it's the light of the moon reflecting on the ocean that leads them from the beach into the ocean, which is their natural habitat. But artificial lights, from homes and hotels, confuse them and can lead them in the wrong direction. As a result, they become more vulnerable to exhaustion and hungry predators, and most of them die before ever making it into the water.

Host: Wow. That is a problem.

Melanie: Right. And sea turtles aren't alone. Many other animal and bird species are affected by light pollution. Migratory birds that travel long distances are another good example. In North America alone, somewhere between one hundred million and one billion birds crash into artificially lit buildings every year. And many of these birds are endangered species. So these losses can be devastating to their survival. And light pollution is totally preventable. Why not do what we can to combat it?

1.3

1 It was first established in 2003 by secondary school student Jennifer Barlow.
2 Large cities obviously produce the most light pollution.
3 Here to tell us more is astronomer Melanie Turow.
4 Astronomers study stars and deep space.
5 But light pollution actually affects all of us.
6 Most of us who live in the city probably never think about it.
7 Baby sea turtles hatch from their eggs on beaches.
8 And light pollution is totally preventable.

UNIT 2

Teacher: Today we're finishing our unit on industrial design; the process of designing products for mass production. Your assignment was to prepare a presentation about a product that has been improved through the industrial design process. We're going to start with Serena.

Serena: Thank you. Before I get started, I'd like you to think about the last time you washed your hands in a public toilet. How did you dry them? Did you use paper towels? Or maybe you used an electric hand dryer? I hope you used a dryer because today I'd like to talk about hand dryers; how design changes have drastically improved this product and made our lives just a little bit easier.

Let's start at the beginning. The first electric hand dryer was invented in 1921 by the Airdry Corporation of New York, who called it the 'electric towel'. The hand dryer gained popularity, thanks to George Clemens, an inventor who was a pioneer in household electronics like the electric toothbrush. His company, World Dryer, began producing hand dryers for shared toilets in public spaces and businesses in 1949 and was the world's largest manufacturer of these machines for almost fifty years. During this time, hand dryers were adopted because of all the advantages they offered over paper towels — they were cheaper, less wasteful, and helped to reduce rubbish.

But, if you've ever used one of these old hand dryers, I'm sure you are aware of their downsides: they were incredibly slow and inefficient. It took people nearly a minute to completely dry their hands — that is, if they didn't get impatient and grab a towel or use their trousers or shirt to finish the job. No one liked using them. Even so, hand dryer technology stayed pretty much the same throughout most of the twentieth century.

Then, in 1993, the Japanese manufacturer Mitsubishi devised a hand dryer that used greater force to blow the water off hands rather than slowly dry them with heat, as the old hand dryers did. This was an improvement, but it didn't really catch on.

The first major advance in hand dryer technology came several years later, when Denis Gagnon, the owner of a company called Excel Dryers, teamed up with a group of retired scientists from MIT to develop a new, faster hand dryer. These scientists knew that the old hand dryers wasted ninety percent of the energy that went into them. They spent three and a half years developing a more efficient dryer and, in 2001, they released the Xlerator, a hand dryer that could dry hands in just twelve seconds, by using a powerful blast of warm air.

Sales of the Xlerator took off, and soon began a horse race for the world's best hand dryer. In 2006, the UK-based company Dyson released an electric hand dryer called the Airblade. Instead of blasting the hands with heated air, the Airblade uses a thin layer of unheated air that travels so fast — around four hundred miles per hour — that it can push water off hands in just ten seconds. Since then, manufacturers have continued to experiment with hand dryer technology to make improvements. Subsequent hand dryers have been developed to be quieter, use less energy, catch dripping water, and accommodate people of different heights. In 2013, Dyson even produced a hand-washer-and-dryer-in-one machine, which completely eliminates water dripping on the floor.

But the biggest obstacle to the use of hand dryers remains the paper towel. Most people, given a choice, still prefer to use paper towels. But we also know that paper towels are much more expensive than modern hand dryers – up to ninety-five percent more expensive. In fact, the cost of paper towels is so much greater than the cost of the electricity needed to run hand dryers, that a hand dryer can pay for itself in just a few months. People today are also more environmentally conscious, and they know that hand dryers are a more responsible option, producing less waste and pollution. They also make public toilets cleaner and easier to maintain.

So, as you can see, even ordinary products like hand dryers can encourage advances in design and engineering and have a big impact on our quality of life.

1 mass production
2 drastically
3 manufacturer
4 downsides
5 inefficient
6 technology
7 devised
8 horse race
9 subsequent

UNIT 3

Alicia: This is Tech Savvy, the podcast that keeps you up to date on the latest in digital technology. I'm Alicia Martinez, your personal tech advisor. On today's show I'm taking a break from my usual focus on cool new innovations to talk about something all tech users should be concerned about: privacy.

If you're like me, you love your personal digital technology. But how personal is it really? There are tradeoffs for these modern conveniences. You want directions to your friend's house? Then you have to enter your current location and agree to be tracked. You want to buy those shoes online? Then your credit card number is in the cloud. Some results of all this public personal information are minor – like those annoying ads constantly popping up for things you already bought – but others can be pretty serious, like identity theft. And who knows in what other ways our personal data could be used against us in the future?

The problem is, too many of us have no idea what we are sharing or agreeing to when we go online. Researchers at York University and the University of Connecticut found this out when they created a fake social app and invited students to sign up for it. In their experiment, seventy-four percent of the students who joined didn't even read the privacy policy. And those who did, obviously didn't read it carefully, because by signing up, they agreed to give up their firstborn child to the social network! How's that for creepy?

I don't mean to scare you, but this should be a wake-up call. We have to be better at protecting our personal data. But how?

I know it can seem overwhelming. So, today I'd like to share with you five simple ways you can protect your privacy.

Number one? Turn on automatic software updates. Probably the most critical thing you can do to counter threats to your privacy is to keep your operating system and software up to date. If you have old software, you're missing the latest protections against hackers and identity thieves. Set your software to update automatically, and you won't have to think about it again.

Number two: use screen locks on all of your devices. Without a screen lock, losing your phone, laptop or tablet not only gives a stranger easy access to any personal information you have stored on that device, but also gives them access to information stored on other connected devices – email, banking information, or social media pages full of personal and family history. Your screen lock should be at least six characters long. And don't use an easy-to-guess sequence of numbers.

And that brings me to number three: make unbreakable passwords. We all know that a strong password is crucial for protecting privacy, but most of us still create passwords that are too easy to figure out. A strong password should be long and random – don't follow a predictable pattern, and don't use personal information. One method is to create a list of random words, for example: 'return guitar chat wide cow nervous'. If you need to, add some numbers, symbols or capital letters. Then, think of a little story to connect the words in your mind. You can also avoid memorizing more than one password by using a password manager – an app that creates and stores different complex passwords for each of your accounts.

Tip number four: stop oversharing! There's no need for you to share your phone number, email or address on social media pages, so delete them. And another thing not to share? Your location. Some apps need to know or track your location, but most apps don't. You can turn off location sharing in your phone's settings.

Finally, number five: cover up your laptop's webcam. Why? Hackers can turn on your computer's camera without your knowledge and secretly record you and your computer activity. To avoid that, do what Facebook CEO Mark Zuckerberg does and place a piece of tape or a sticky note over the camera lens.

So, there's my list. Of course, there are plenty of other things you can do to avoid security breaches, but these should get you started. For more tips, visit our web page.

🔊 **3.2**

1 If you're like me, you love your personal digital technology.
2 In their experiment, seventy-four percent of the students who joined didn't even read the privacy policy.
3 We have to be better at protecting our personal data.
4 So, today I'd like to share with you five simple ways you can protect your privacy.
5 Probably the most critical thing you can do to counter threats to your privacy is to keep your operating system and software up to date.
6 Your screen lock should be at least six characters long.
7 You can turn off location sharing in your phone's settings.

🔊 3.3

1 There are tradeoffs for these modern conveniences.
2 You want to buy those shoes online?
3 Then your credit card number is in the cloud.
4 Set your software to update automatically.
5 Use screen locks on all of your devices.
6 A strong password should be long and random.
7 If you need to, add some numbers, symbols or capital letters.
8 You can turn off location sharing in your phone's settings.

UNIT 4

Professor: Today we're talking about corporations. Let me start by asking you – what do you think a corporation is exactly? Yes?

Student 1: A business. A big business – like Microsoft, or Toyota.

Professor: Well, corporations are usually businesses, but not always. Non-profits can also be corporations. And they don't have to be big. In order to achieve corporate status, an organization needs to be independent. In other words, a corporation is an organization that is legally separate from the people who own and run it. A corporation is considered a 'legal person' because it can enter into contracts, loan and borrow money, hire employees, buy property, and pay taxes – just like a person.

But the goal of a corporation depends on the type of organization it is. The mission of non-profit corporations, of course, is to provide some kind of social good. Most corporations, however, are businesses, whose goal is to turn a profit – to make money.

In fact, since the 1970s, most for-profit corporations have followed the thinking of economist Milton Friedman, who considered increasing profits to be the 'only social responsibility of business'. This principle has resulted in some corporations making a lot of money. But, can you think of any potential downsides to this way of thinking?

Student 2: Well, yeah, if profit is all that matters, a company wouldn't care about their workers very much.

Student 1: Yeah, or taking care of the environment.

Professor: Right. Maximizing profits is great for shareholders – that is, the investors who make money through owning shares in the company. But that can come at a cost to other stakeholders – meaning those who are affected by the actions of a corporation. Stakeholders include shareholders, but they also include a company's workforce, the workers' families, the people in the community affected by the success or failure of the company, other businesses that have partnerships with the company – you get the picture.

Many business owners feel it is important to take stakeholders' interests into consideration as well. They want to make a profit and do good beyond the factory walls. So, in 2007, a new type of corporation, called a 'benefit corporation', or B corp, was created to help business owners do just that. A benefit corporation is a for-profit corporation that is required by law to achieve a positive impact – on its workers, the community, society, and the environment – in addition to making a profit. So, unlike a traditional corporation, which is only judged by its financial performance, a B corp is judged by its social, environmental and financial performance.

Student 1: So, how do they do that? I mean, it's easy to measure profits, but how can shareholders judge whether a corporation is having a positive effect on society or the environment?

Professor: Good question. B corps are required by law to publish annual reports of their social and environmental performance, and they are certified by an independent non-profit group called B Lab. B Lab provides oversight and verifies that businesses are meeting their standards. Since 2007, the number of B corps has risen steadily. Chances are you've bought something from one – Etsy, Patagonia, Seventh Generation cleaning products, Ben & Jerry's ice cream. They're all certified B corps.

Student 2: OK, I think it's great that a company would want to do good, but why go to all the trouble of becoming a certified B corp? What's in it for the business?

Professor: Well, for one thing, becoming a certified B corp can help businesses stick to their mission. Shareholders may want them to put profits first, but B corps are legally bound to give equal attention to their social mission.

Becoming a certified B corp can also increase sales. Consumers like to buy products from companies that they can trust. Some companies claim to be socially or environmentally conscious and use buzzwords like 'green' or 'natural' in their advertising, but B corp certification assures customers that a company is living up to its promises.

And another benefit of becoming a B corp – attracting talented employees. Surveys have shown that many young people want to work for companies that have a social mission, and they are willing to accept lower salaries to work for a company they can feel good about.

4.2

1 In other words, a corporation is an organization that is legally separate from the people who own and run it.
2 Most corporations, however, are businesses, whose goal is to turn a profit – to make money.
3 Maximizing profits is great for shareholders – that is, the investors who make money through owning shares in the company.
4 But that can come at a cost to other stakeholders – meaning those who are affected by the actions of a corporation.
5 A benefit corporation is a for-profit corporation that is required by law to achieve a positive impact – on its workers, the community, society, and the environment – in addition to making a profit.

4.3

1 A corporation is considered a 'legal person' because it can enter into contracts, loan and borrow money, hire employees, buy property, and pay taxes – just like a person.
2 The mission of non-profit corporations, of course, is to provide some kind of social good.
3 In fact, since the 1970s, most for-profit corporations have followed the thinking of economist Milton Friedman, who considered increasing profits to be the 'only social responsibility of business'.
4 Maximizing profits is great for shareholders – that is, the investors who make money through owning shares in the company.

5 So, in 2007, a new type of corporation, called a 'benefit corporation', or B corp, was created to help business owners do just that.

6 Some companies claim to be socially or environmentally conscious and use buzzwords like 'green' or 'natural' in their advertising, but B corp certification assures customers that a company is living up to its promises.

UNIT 5

Professor: Next, I'd like to talk about ADHD – Attention Deficit Hyperactivity Disorder – one of the most common brain disorders that affects children.

So what is ADHD? According to the National Institute of Mental Health, ADHD is defined as a 'brain disorder marked by an ongoing pattern of inattention and/or hyperactivity-impulsivity that interferes with functioning or development'.

Let's look at the symptoms, or behavioural cues, associated with ADHD: inattention, hyperactivity, and impulsivity. First of all, inattention. Inattention describes someone who has trouble focusing on a task. Children with inattention are easily distracted and make careless mistakes in schoolwork or other activities. They also may have difficulty following instructions and staying organized.

Hyperactivity describes children who are overly active. Hyperactive children seem to be constantly 'on the move', have difficulty sitting still, and may talk too much.

Finally, impulsivity describes someone who acts before thinking about the result of their actions. Impulsive children often have difficulty waiting their turn and may interrupt others.

So, how is ADHD diagnosed, or recognized, by a doctor or a psychologist? First, we gather information from at least two sources, such as parents and teachers, to verify the child has shown several symptoms of ADHD for at least six months. The symptoms of ADHD need to have been present before the child was twelve, and the symptoms must impair the child's functioning in two or more settings, such as at home and at school. And finally, there must be clear evidence that these symptoms aren't caused by another mental disorder. In short, ADHD is not a simple condition to diagnose.

In general, children with ADHD have problems with inattention, hyperactivity, and impulsivity. But some may have trouble with only one of the behaviours, and the symptoms can change over time. In pre-school aged children, hyperactivity-impulsivity is usually the primary concern, whereas inattention and impulsivity are bigger problems for teens and may continue into adulthood.

So, what causes ADHD? The bottom line is we don't know for sure. There are a number of possible factors. One factor is genetics. ADHD can run in families. Environment is another possible influence. Some speculate that exposure to drugs, alcohol, or smoking during pregnancy can lead to ADHD in the baby, just as exposure to environmental toxins – such as lead paint – can cause it in children. Another risk factor is premature birth, which can negatively affect brain development.

Overall, while we don't know the exact cause of ADHD, we do know that ADHD can be successfully treated. One treatment is behaviour therapy, in which children are taught new behaviours to replace behaviours that are destructive or disruptive. Parents can also benefit from learning ways to help manage their child's behaviour.

Another common treatment is medication. About two-thirds of children with ADHD use prescription medication, such as Ritalin or Adderall. Medications can be quite effective in treating ADHD, helping children to focus and reduce their disruptive behaviours, and perform better in school. But these medications can have side effects, such as sleep difficulties, headaches, stomach aches and loss of appetite. There are also concerns that medications can lead to more serious effects, such as heart problems, anxiety and addiction.

ADHD is a big problem that is growing bigger: the number of children diagnosed with the disorder is rising. In 2011, twelve percent of US children and teens had a diagnosis of ADHD. That was a forty-three percent increase since 2003 and amounted to six point four million children between the ages of four and seventeen.

So what's causing this increase? Some believe there is no increase. We just have a name now for something that has always existed. Others speculate that ADHD is a consequence of poor sleeping habits or exposure to electronics, or the result of not enough time spent playing outdoors. Others worry that the increase is due to the pressure put on kids from schools and parents to improve academic performance. As a result, doctors may be too quick to diagnose ADHD and prescribe medications to people who don't need it.

To sum up, it's clear that ADHD is a problem that requires further research to help us better understand its causes and develop more effective prevention and treatment options.

🔊 **5.2**

Professor: So, what causes ADHD? The bottom line is we don't know for sure. There are a number of possible factors. One factor is genetics. ADHD can run in families. Environment is another possible influence. Some speculate that exposure to drugs, alcohol, or smoking during pregnancy can lead to ADHD in the baby, just as exposure to environmental toxins – such as lead paint – can cause it in children. Another risk factor is premature birth, which can negatively affect brain development.

🔊 **5.3**

Professor: So what's causing this increase? Some believe there is no increase. We just have a name now for something that has always existed. Others speculate that ADHD is a consequence of poor sleeping habits or exposure to electronics, or the result of not enough time spent playing outdoors. Others worry that the increase is due to the pressure put on kids from schools and parents to improve academic performance. As a result, doctors may be too quick to diagnose ADHD and prescribe medications to people who don't need it.

1 So what is ADHD?
2 First of all, inattention.
3 Children with inattention are easily distracted and make careless mistakes in schoolwork or other activities.
4 They also may have difficulty following instructions and staying organized.
5 Hyperactivity describes children who are overly active.
6 Hyperactive children seem to be constantly 'on the move', have difficulty sitting still, and may talk too much.
7 Finally, impulsivity describes someone who acts before thinking about the result of their actions.
8 Impulsive children often have difficulty waiting their turn and may interrupt others.

UNIT 6

Josh: Hey, Eva!

Eva: Hi, Josh!

Josh: Wow, I don't think I've seen you since graduation. How's it going?

Eva: Great! I got a job. I started about two months ago.

Josh: That's great! What are you doing?

Eva: I'm a computer programmer for a small tech company in the city centre. It's been challenging, but I'm learning so much, and the people are great.

Josh: That's awesome! Hey, tell me about your interview. I'm working for my dad right now in his shop, but I've got an interview with a big marketing company next week, and I want to [wanna] know what to expect. What did they ask you?

Eva: Well, the interviewer started off by just saying 'Tell me about yourself,' which seems like an easy enough question, right? But you have to [hafta] be careful not to ramble on and on, without talking about what they really want to [wanna] know. Luckily, I'd met with a careers adviser, and he helped me prepare.

Josh: So, how did you answer?

Eva: Well, first I introduced myself and gave her a short summary of my accomplishments – I talked about the computer programs I know and a project I worked on in school that fitted with the kinds of things they do. The careers adviser had ['d] suggested researching the company and the position before the interview so I could [kud] talk about how my skills and experience matched their needs. He said that even though interviewers ask you to talk about yourself, what they really want to [wanna] know is what you can do for them.

Josh: Yeah, that makes sense.

Eva: So before the interview I read the company's website, and I searched for reviews and articles about it. The company's pretty new. They're growing quickly and going through a lot of changes. I even found a friend of a friend who works there and could tell me what it's like on the inside, what the company culture is like.

Josh: Wow! It sounds like you really did your homework. So what else did the interviewer ask you?

Eva: Well, she asked the 'biggest strength' question, of course, so, knowing something about the company, I figured they'd be looking for employees who can switch gears quickly and cope with different types of projects. So I said, my biggest strength is being adaptable, you know, good at dealing with change, handling things as they come up. I told her about a time when I was working on a group project for class, and one of my teammates was ill and I had to jump in, work out his part, and get it done myself. I could [kud] tell she liked my answer. It really paid to have some specific examples prepared.

Josh: Huh. I would have [uv] thought they'd care more about being analytical, or good with technical stuff, you know, for a computer programmer.

Eva: Well, technical skills are important, but even tech companies are looking for employees with great soft skills.

Josh: Soft skills?

Eva: Yeah, soft skills are personal skills that help you get along with other people and just be an all-round good employee – stuff like being hardworking, having integrity, you know, being honest and dependable, or having good collaboration skills. Those kinds of skills are always going to [gonna] help you, no matter what job you do.

Josh: Good to know. I'll think about my soft skills. So, what else did she ask?

Eva: She also asked, 'Why do you [Why'd'you] want this job?' That question gave me the chance to show how informed I was about their company, that I cared enough to do research. I told her what I knew and liked about the company and the position – and how I was excited to help a small company grow. I could tell she was impressed that I'd thought about what made me a good fit. Hey, sorry Josh, I've got to [gotta] run, but good luck with your interview next week. Let me know how it goes. OK?

Josh: Yeah, cool, I will. Thanks. And congratulations on the job. That's really great.

6.2

1 Well, the interviewer started off by just saying 'Tell me about yourself,' which seems like an easy enough question, right?
2 But you have to be careful not to ramble on and on, without talking about what they really want to know. Luckily, I'd met with a careers adviser, and he helped me prepare.
3 Wow! It sounds like you really did your homework.
4 So, knowing something about the company, I figured they'd be looking for employees who can switch gears quickly and cope with different types of projects.
5 Huh. I would have thought they'd care more about being analytical, or good with technical stuff.

6.3

1 I want to [wanna] know what to expect.
2 You have to [hafta] be careful not to ramble on and on, without talking about what they really want to [wanna] know.
3 The careers adviser had ['d] suggested researching the company and the position before the interview.
4 I could [kud] talk about how my skills and experience matched their needs.
5 What they really want to [wanna] know is what you can do for them.
6 I could [kud] tell she liked my answer.
7 I would have [uv] thought they'd care more about being analytical.
8 Those kinds of skills are always going to [gonna] help you, no matter what job you do.
9 She also asked, 'Why do you [Why'd'you] want this job?'

UNIT 7

Host: Today we have a guest speaker, Doctor Amit Kumar, an ear, nose and throat specialist, who's here to talk to us about hearing loss. Now, if you're like me, you are probably thinking that hearing loss is an old person's problem and not something we need to be concerned about. But, actually, that's not the case.

Dr Kumar: No, it isn't. We all know the stereotype of the elderly person who is hard of hearing, but ironically, the majority of people with hearing loss are younger than sixty-five. And the incidence of hearing loss is growing in young people at an alarming rate. Today, the rate of hearing loss in teens is thirty percent higher than it was in the 1990s. Nearly one in five teens suffers from some hearing loss.

Host: Today we have a guest speaker, Doctor Amit Kumar, an ear, nose and throat specialist, who's here to talk to us about hearing loss. Now, if you're like me, you are probably thinking that hearing loss is an old person's problem and not something we need to be concerned about. But, actually, that's not the case.

Dr Kumar: No, it isn't. We all know the stereotype of the elderly person who is hard of hearing, but ironically, the majority of people with hearing loss are younger than sixty-five. And the incidence of hearing loss is growing in young people at an alarming rate. Today, the rate of hearing loss in teens is thirty percent higher than it was in the 1990s. Nearly one in five teens suffers from some hearing loss.

Host: So we really do need to hear about this problem – if we can, that is.

Dr Kumar: Absolutely. Let me start with an overview of the two main types of hearing loss, and then we'll move on to ways to prevent it. The first type, conductive hearing loss, happens when sound can't travel efficiently down the outer ear canal through the middle ear – for instance, when there is fluid in the middle ear. This type of hearing loss reduces the intensity, or volume, of sound, making it difficult to hear quiet noises. If you've ever had an ear infection or bad allergies, you've probably experienced this type of hearing impairment.

The second type, sensorineural hearing loss, occurs when there is damage to the inner ear or the nerve pathways in and out of it. Some of the causes include genetics, ageing, or exposure to loud noise. Unlike conductive hearing loss, sensorineural hearing loss can result in sounds being unclear, even when they are loud enough.

It's the second type of hearing loss, sensorineural, that I'd like to focus on today, since this is the type that is increasing the most in young people. And unlike conductive hearing loss, which can often be corrected with surgery or medication, sensorineural hearing loss typically can't be corrected and results in permanent loss of hearing. Really, the only treatment for this type of hearing loss is the use of hearing aids to make sounds louder.

But fortunately, this type of hearing loss can often be prevented simply by reducing exposure to noise. Noise is one of the most common causes of hearing loss, because we can easily expose ourselves to damaging noise – at work, at home, anywhere – and because the loss is often gradual, we don't realize the harm we've done until it's too late.

Host: So how can we know if noise is safe or not?

Dr Kumar: Well, first it helps to understand decibels – the unit of measure for sound. A normal conversation is about sixty decibels, while noise from heavy city traffic is about eighty-five decibels. Noise levels at or below seventy-five decibels are considered safe for adults, but at eighty-five decibels, exposure should be limited to no more than eight hours. And once you get up to a hundred decibels, which is about the level of an MP3 player at maximum volume, you're causing damage after only fifteen minutes. So the louder the sound, the shorter the amount of time it takes for damage to occur.

Host: Wow, so does that mean we need to give up our music players?

Dr Kumar: Well, there's no need to deprive yourself of your favourite tunes, but I do recommend the sixty-sixty rule for using personal audio devices: limit the volume to no more than sixty percent of maximum volume, and listen for no more than sixty minutes a day. It's also helpful to use over-the-ear headphones instead of earbuds. Earbuds can be more damaging because they place the sound closer to the ear drum. And, because they are not as good at filtering out other noises, you are more likely to turn the volume up to an unsafe level. And another piece of advice: if you're going to a loud concert, be sure to wear earplugs. You'll thank yourself someday.

 7.3

1 We all know the stereotype of the elderly person who is hard of hearing, but ironically, the majority of people with hearing loss are younger than sixty-five.
2 Today, the rate of hearing loss in teens is thirty percent higher than it was in the 1990s.
3 Unlike conductive hearing loss, sensorineural hearing loss can result in sounds being unclear, even when they are loud enough.
4 A normal conversation is about sixty decibels, while noise from heavy city traffic is about eight-five decibels.

UNIT 8
 8.1

Presenter: We all know that collaboration is highly valued in our society. As students, we are constantly asked to work in groups or with a partner. And more and more workplaces are requiring their employees to work in teams. Researchers have found that collaboration at work has increased by at least fifty percent in the last twenty years.

But is that a good thing? Let's take a poll. If you were given the choice of doing a project in a group or on your own, how many of you would prefer to work alone? Be honest ... OK, I can see that many of you agree with that old expression 'too many cooks spoil the broth'.

Today, I'd like to present three downsides to working collaboratively and explain why I think we should recognize the benefits of working alone.

OK, downside number one: working collaboratively is not efficient. People learn and work at different speeds. We've all seen this: if a group moves too fast for a member, that person can get left behind and not learn anything. Or, if the group slows down to explain things, the whole group falls behind.

And people don't work as hard in a group as they do on their own. In one recent study, psychologists found that people form more solid memories when they believe they are the only one doing a task. One explanation for this is the idea of 'social loafing'. This is a concept in social psychology that says that people tend not to try as hard if they think they can rely on others who also have a stake in the work. When we collaborate, we also tend to get distracted by other group members' thoughts and opinions. A lot of time is wasted trying to resolve disagreements and build consensus, not to mention getting off track and just chatting. When we work alone, we can stay focused on achieving the goal.

Which leads me to downside number two: working collaboratively is not effective. Supporters of collaboration often say 'two heads are better than one'. But another recent study found that collaboration sometimes gets in the way of problem solving. People in groups tend to copy one another and agree more. This results in fewer and potentially worse solutions than if people were to work on their own. Other research shows that teams tend to develop a 'group mind', and outcomes depend more on how well the group members get along than on their intelligence or skill. So, group dynamics often get in the way of great ideas. Think about history-changing innovations, creative works, or scientific discoveries. Chances are they came from the mind of an individual.

And the third downside: collaboration is not fair. If you've ever been in a group where the other members didn't pull their own weight, then you'll know what I mean. There is always someone who doesn't do their fair share of the work, leaving the others to pick up the slack. Researchers conducted a study across more than three hundred organizations and found that up to one-third of successful collaborations came from only three to five percent of employees. The people who are the most capable and willing to help end up being given a disproportionate amount of work. They then suffer from what the researchers call 'success syndrome', meaning sooner or later they burn out and quit. Group dynamics can also be unfair to quieter group members. Shy people can be ignored and not have their ideas heard. Too much socializing can also drain the energy of shy people, leading them to feel tired and overwhelmed.

Having said all that, I do want to stress that there's no need to 'throw the baby out with the bath water'. Too much isolation is not healthy, and collaboration does have value, especially for certain tasks like brainstorming. But let's not forget the important contributions of the individual and the value of working alone.

🔊 8.2

1 I can see that many of you agree with that old expression 'too many cooks spoil the broth'.
2 Supporters of collaboration often say 'two heads are better than one'. But a recent study found that collaboration sometimes gets in the way of problem solving.
3 If you've ever been in a group where the other members didn't pull their own weight, then you'll know what I mean.
4 There is always someone who doesn't do their fair share of the work, leaving the others to pick up the slack.
5 They then suffer from what the researchers call 'success syndrome', meaning sooner or later they burn out and quit.
6 I do want to stress that there's no need to 'throw the baby out with the bath water'. Too much isolation is not healthy, and collaboration does have value, especially for certain tasks like brainstorming.

🔊 8.3

1 It'll take longer to reach consensus than it will to decide individually.
2 I know what'll happen if we work together. I'll end up doing most of the work.
3 Maybe the others won't help, but I will. We'll finish it together.
4 A: Will you please give me a hand with this?
   B: I can't, but I'm sure Paul will once he gets home.
5 Our group'll report our results tomorrow. When'll your group be ready?

UNIT 9

Presenter: Good morning and welcome to today's programme. Today we're going to be talking about the Internet of Things. Today's guest is Paul Honeycomb, who is a professor of Computer Networking. Paul, what can you tell us about the Internet of Things?

Paul: Yeah, OK, so as you know, the internet is expanding rapidly and is no longer limited to computers. More and more devices are being connected to the internet and it is estimated that within the next few years, there will be well over fifty billion internet-connected devices around the world. This is known as the Internet of Things. The Internet of Things refers to everyday objects which are connected to the internet, allowing them to send and receive data.

Presenter: Could you be more specific about the kinds of devices that might be connected to the internet?

Paul: Well, let's look at an example: most people have heard of smartwatches or fitness trackers. Smartwatches function both as watches and as computers, so we can use these to read emails or surf the internet. They can also function as GPS devices to guide us from A to B. Fitness trackers measure how many steps you have walked, how many calories you have burned or how much exercise you have done. Some of them connect to your smartphone or computer via Bluetooth, but the more advanced ones connect directly to the internet to upload your data. This seems like a natural progression, but what would you think of controlling your heating or your washing machine via the internet?

Presenter: Do you mean that you can control your washing machine from your smartphone?

Paul: Actually, yes, you can! Modern household devices – for instance, lights, heating, kettles and washing machines – allow you to control them via the internet. The devices connect to the internet via your home Wi-Fi network and you control them remotely via your smartphone.

Presenter: I see.

Paul: Other internet-connected devices include doorbells and CCTV cameras which enable you to see who is at your door or on your property and open the door remotely if you so desire.

There are also devices for cars which can track the state of your car and diagnose problems with it. They can also locate the position of your car and notify relatives in the case of an accident.

If you need a car, in some places you can even hire a car via your smartphone. Cars are located in different parts of a city and, using your smartphone, you enter the car's details, access the key in the key store and off you go. There is no need to go to the office to pick up the key and sign the papers.

Presenter: Well, all of these internet-connected devices may sound fabulous but there must be some drawbacks?

Paul: You know, as with all technology, there are benefits and drawbacks to consider.

One major benefit, clearly, is convenience. Being able to see who is at your house when you are out allows you to take delivery of goods without receiving one of those irritating cards saying 'We called but you were out' and then having to rearrange delivery. Instead, you can talk to the delivery driver and tell them where to leave the package.

Another positive aspect is safety. Knowing that your car's performance is being monitored provides you with the security of knowing that you will be alerted before anything goes wrong.

However, there are also drawbacks and security is one of them. Every internet-connected device is an additional risk to the security of your network and your privacy. All the devices have an ID tag which provides information about the device but can also provide information about you, which can be very useful to companies who want to monitor consumers' activities or interests.

Another drawback is the potential digital divide between those who know how the technology works and those who don't. The risk is that some people will adopt the Internet of Things and will understand how everything works while others, who are not so technologically capable, will be left behind.

Presenter: Hmm, that sounds very interesting. Thanks for explaining that. OK, listeners, we would now be interested in hearing your opinions about the Internet of Things. Is it a positive development or is it a dangerous road we are going down? …

Lecturer: I hope you all had a chance to read the articles for today's seminar. With the recent advances in robotics, the issue of AI taking over human jobs has caused a great deal of concern. We all know that robots work in factory assembly lines, manufacturing cars and computer chips. In some places, robots are used as prison guards. Restaurants in different parts of the world employ robots to take orders and serve food. Humanoid robots have been used to man reception desks and interact with customers.

9.3

1 A: 'Trainphobes' thought that trains would cause people's organs to explode if they travelled on trains.
B: Are you saying that people thought trains were so fast that our bodies would not be able to cope with the high speeds?

2 A: My parents usually control our heating from their phone so the house is always warm when we get home.
B: I'm not sure I understand. Would you elaborate, please?

3 A: I don't think humanoid robots will ever be as capable as humans.
B: What do you mean by saying that humanoid robots will never be as capable as humans?

4 A: In my opinion, humans will only be employable if they are capable of designing better robots and better technology.
B: Do you mean that if we are not computer programmers, inventors or designers, we will be unemployable in the future?

5 A: You can have a device in your car which will constantly monitor your car and will tell you if there is a problem so you don't break down in the middle of the road.
B: Are you saying that your car will actually tell you that something is about to break before it does, so you have time to get to a garage?

6 A: If we control so many things via smartphone, it would be a true disaster if the phone broke or was lost.
B: Sorry, but could you be a bit more explicit?

UNIT 10

Lecturer: Good morning, everyone. Welcome to this week's session. Today we are going to be looking at the origins of words so, to start with, I would like you to get into groups of three or four different nationalities and I would like you to discuss whether you know any words in English that come from your language. I'll give you about five minutes to discuss that as a group.

Javier: So, I know English is a Germanic language but it has a lot of influence from Romance languages like Latin and French, as does Spanish – but Spanish also has a lot of Moorish Arabic influence, too. For example, in Spanish, we use the Arabic word 'Alhambra', which literally means 'The Red One' but it is used in English, too, as it is the name of the Moorish palace in Granada.

Natasha: Are there any other words related to history used in English?

Khalid: Yeah, there are Arabic words like 'sultan' and 'mummy', of course. 'Sultan' is a title for a ruler but 'mummy' (in the sense of a dead body which has been preserved, you know, like the ancient Egyptians did) comes from 'mumiya'.

Natasha: Oh, that is exactly the same in Russian: 'mumiya'! And it is very similar in German, too: 'Mumie'. What about other words? Anything related to transport?

Khalid: Well, there is 'tare', you know, like 'tare weight'? That comes from the Medieval Arabic: 'tarh' or 'tarha'.

Javier: Sorry, could I just stop you there? What does 'tare weight' mean? I have never heard of it.

Khalid: The tare weight of something is the weight of something when it is empty. For example, a lorry will have a tare weight – a weight when it is empty, and a gross weight – the weight of a lorry and its load.

Javier: Oh, that has just reminded me of another Spanish word: 'cargo' – you know, like freight. That comes from the Spanish verb 'cargar', which means 'to carry'.

Natasha: In Russian we have words related to space travel such as 'cosmonaut' – which originally comes from the Greek word 'cosmos' and 'nautes' meaning 'sailors'– and 'sputnik', which relates to the Soviet space satellites. We also have some political words such as 'perestroika', 'glasnost' and 'Bolshevik' ...

Javier: And in Spanish we have 'embargo' ...

Khalid: Sorry, could I just stop you there? I have heard the word 'embargo' but I am not sure what it is. Can you explain it?

Javier: Yes, it comes from the Spanish word 'embargar', which means 'to hinder', so an embargo is a restriction on trade – for example, that a government of one country might impose on another country as a punishment.

Khalid: Good. What about food or drink?

Javier: There are lots of Spanish words for food in English: 'paella', 'fajitas', 'tapas' ... 'Cafeteria' is a Spanish word which is used in English, but it is usually shortened to café.

Khalid: 'Sugar' and 'alcohol' are Arabic in origin.

Natasha: I didn't realize that those were Arabic words, but I'd like to pick up on what Javier was saying about 'cafeteria' or 'café'. I think 'café' has become an international word because we have the same word in Russian and I believe it is used in other languages, too. For example, French and German ...

Javier: Yes, that's right. What about animals? I can think of 'armadillo' from Spanish. That comes from 'armado', which means 'armed' and the diminutive '-illo', meaning 'small'. An armadillo is a mammal with hard plates on its back – hence 'armed'.

Khalid: 'Giraffe' and 'gazelle' come from Arabic ...

Natasha: Yes, that reminds me of 'beluga' for the beluga whale and 'mammoth', the large prehistoric mammal ...

Javier: Sorry to interrupt you – I just wanted to say that we have 'beluga' in Spanish, too. 'Ballena beluga' means 'beluga whale'.

Natasha: Great. Anything else?

Khalid: The only other thing I can think of is 'check', from 'shah' and 'checkmate' from 'shah mat'. 'Shah' is a Persian word for 'king', and 'shah mat' is Medieval Arabic, meaning 'king dead'.

Natasha: Really? In Russian we say 'shakh i mat', and German uses 'schachmatt' for 'checkmate' so they must be borrowed directly from the Arabic, too, I suppose.

Khalid: It sounds like it, yes.

Lecturer: Ok, everyone, let me stop you there …

10.2

Mary: I remember that I had Russian friends visiting once. I wanted to send them directions to my house. I used an internet translation app to translate my directions from English to Russian and then I sent them to my friends. I can't read Russian so I had no idea what it said.

10.3

Lecturer: That is an excellent example. Vocabulary-related problems account for the biggest setbacks in the development of machine translation. In fact, being able to determine which sense or meaning of a word to use has been one of the biggest challenges faced by scientists involved in developing machine translation programmes since the 1950s. IBM was the first company to launch a machine translation programme, known as 'the brain'. In those days, IBM scientists claimed that to translate a small section of text required more programming than it took to simulate the flight of a guided missile.

10.4

Speaker 1: I was just reading about the Critical Age Hypothesis. Have you heard of it? It suggests that there is a certain age after which it is impossible to learn a language to a native-like proficiency. The research evidence is really fascinating. I'm not sure whether I agree with it or not.

Speaker 2: Are you saying that we can only learn language to a high level if we're below a certain age?

Speaker 1: Well, that's what the theory suggests. As I was saying, the research evidence is fascinating but there are arguments on both sides. Some researchers argue that the critical age can be as low as three, for example, to get a perfect accent, but others argue it may be around age thirteen. Opponents of the Critical Age Hypothesis suggest it is linked to other factors such as time available to learn and motivation.

Speaker 3: If I could just come in here, I'm not clear on the age range. How can some people argue that the critical age is three while others say it is thirteen?

Speaker 1: Researchers look at different aspects of language learning – for example, pronunciation, where they say the age is younger, or grammatical features, where the age is higher. What I was trying to say is that there are interesting studies for both sides of the argument …

Speaker 2: I'm sorry to interrupt you but I'm not convinced that there is a critical age. I know a lot of adults who speak foreign languages very well – to the point that you wouldn't know they were non-native speakers.

Speaker 3: Yes, but they don't usually have a perfect accent – you can usually tell they are non-native speakers. On the other hand, people who have grown up in the country usually have a perfect native-speaker accent.

Speaker 1: That was precisely the point I was making – that there are plausible arguments on both sides …

ACKNOWLEDGEMENTS

The authors and publishers acknowledge the following sources of copyright material and are grateful for the permissions granted. While every effort has been made, it has not always been possible to identify the sources of all the material used, or to trace all copyright holders. If any omissions are brought to our notice, we will be happy to include the appropriate acknowledgements on reprinting and in the next update to the digital edition, as applicable.

Photo acknowledgements

Key: T = Top, L = Left, C = Centre, R = Right, B = Below.

p. 4 (T): cuiphoto/iStock/Getty Images Plus/Getty Images; p. 4 (B): Mendowong Photography/Moment/Getty Images; p. 10: photogress/E+/Getty Images; p. 12 (L): Jackie Goodman/EyeEm/Getty Images; p. 12 (C): Ramonespelt/iStock/Getty Images Plus/Getty Images; p. 12 (R): View Pictures/Universal Images Group/Getty Images; p. 18 (L): Martin Pickard/Moment/Getty Images; p. 18 (R): Tom Merton/OJO Images/Getty Images; p. 25: Andrew Brookes/Cultura/Getty Images; p. 28: Jacobs Stock Photography/Photodisc/Getty Images Plus/Getty Images; p. 34: Westend61/Getty Images; p. 36: pixdeluxe/iStock/Getty Images Plus/Getty Images; p. 50 (photo 1): Compassionate Eye Foundation/Justin Pumfrey/Iconica/Getty Images; p. 50 (photo 2): innovatedcaptures/iStock/Getty Images Plus/Getty Images; p. 50 (photo 3): Robert Daly/OJO Images/Getty Images; p. 50 (photo 4): Dan Dalton/Caiaimage/Getty Images; p. 51 (photo a): asiseeit/E+/Getty Images; p. 51 (photo b): Deagreez/iStock/Getty Images Plus/Getty Images; p. 51 (photo c): Image Source/Getty Images; p. 51 (photo d): Digital Vision/Getty Images; p. 52 (L): Thinkstock/Stockbyte/Getty Images; p. 52 (R): pixdeluxe/E+/Getty Images; p. 58: webphotographeer/E+/Getty Images; p. 60: alvarez/E+/Getty Images; p. 61: Samir Hussein/WireImage/Getty Images; p. 68 (L): MacFormat Magazine/Future Publishing/Getty Images; p. 68 (C): mikkelwilliam/E+/Getty Images; p. 68 (R): felixmizioznikov/iStock Editorial/Getty Images Plus/Getty Images.

Cover Photography by Stringer/AFP/Getty Images.

Corpus

Development of this publication has made use of the Cambridge English Corpus (CEC). The CEC is a multi-billion word computer database of contemporary spoken and written English. It includes British English, American English, and other varieties of English. It also includes the Cambridge Learner Corpus, developed in collaboration with the University of Cambridge ESOL Examinations. Cambridge University Press has built up the CEC to provide evidence about language use that helps to produce better language teaching materials

Cambridge Dictionaries

Cambridge dictionaries are the world's most widely used dictionaries for learners of English. The dictionaries are available in print and online at dictionary.cambridge.org. Copyright © Cambridge University Press, reproduced with permission.

URLs

The publisher has used its best endeavours to ensure that the URLs for external websites referred to in this book are correct and active at the time of going to press. However, the publisher has no responsibility for the websites and can make no guarantee that a site will remain live or that the content is or will remain appropriate.

Typeset by emc design ltd.

Audio production by The Soundhouse London